KISS THE EYES OF PEACE

KISS THE EYES OF PEACE

SELECTED POEMS 1964–2014

TOMAŽ ŠALAMUN

Edited and translated from the Slovenian

by **BRIAN HENRY**

Foreword by **ILYA KAMINSKY**

MILKWEED EDITIONS

Published 2024 by Milkweed Editions
Printed in Canada
Cover design by Mary Austin Speaker
Author photo by Jože Suhadolnik
Translator photo by Tara Rebele
24 25 26 27 28   5 4 3 2 1
First Edition

Library of Congress Cataloging-in-Publication Data

Names: Šalamun, Tomaž, author. | Henry, Brian, 1972- translator.
Title: Kiss the eyes of peace : selected poems, 1964-2014 / Tomaž
    Šalamun; edited and translated from the Slovenian by Brian Henry.
Description: First edition. | Minneapolis, Minnesota : Milkweed Editions,
    2024. | Summary: "An authoritative volume representing the vast oeuvre
    of one of the twentieth century's most brilliant and visionary poets"--
    Provided by publisher.
Identifiers: LCCN 2023033721 (print) | LCCN 2023033722 (ebook) | ISBN
    9781639550401 (hardcover ; acid-free paper) | ISBN 9781639550814
    (e-book)
Subjects: LCSH: Šalamun, Tomaž--Translations into English. | LCGFT:
    Poetry.
Classification: LCC PG1919.29.A5 K56 2024 (print) | LCC PG1919.29.A5
    (ebook) | DDC 891.8/415--dc23/eng/20231206
LC record available at https://lccn.loc.gov/2023033721
LC ebook record available at https://lccn.loc.gov/2023033722

Milkweed Editions is committed to ecological stewardship. We strive to align our book
production practices with this principle, and to reduce the impact of our operations in
the environment. We are a member of the Green Press Initiative, a nonprofit coalition
of publishers, manufacturers, and authors working to protect the world's endangered
forests and conserve natural resources. *Kiss the Eyes of Peace* was printed on acid-free 100%
postconsumer-waste paper by Friesens Corporation.

CONTENTS

Sonnet About Milk (1984)

Soy Realidad (1985)

Ljubljana Spring (1986)

The Measure of Time (1987)

Living Wound, Living Juice (1988)

The Child and the Deer (1990)

Ambergris (1995)

Black Swan (1997)

Book for My Brother (1997)

FOREWORD
PAN-ŠALAMUNIAN RELIGION

Absurdist

The poet Tomaž Šalamun did not like to speak about his five days in Yugoslav prison.

When he was twenty-three years old, Šalamun wrote a poem calling his countrymen "ideologues with whorish ideologies," "trained intellectuals with sweaty hands," and "rectors with muzzles." None of that got him in trouble.

What got him in trouble was the dead cat mentioned in the middle of the piece. The Interior Minister, whose last name literally meant "cat," took it personally. "He felt that he was attacked personally, and he put me in jail,"[1] Šalamun later recalled, which caused an international uproar. Freed, Šalamun did the unexpected, refusing to reprint the poem in any of his books. When asked why, he said, "Others suffered much more than I did."

But this tale doesn't end there.

After being released from prison, Šalamun was barred from holding any government job (and in Yugoslavia, most jobs were government jobs). So he walked door-to-door, selling black-market encyclopedias. Once, he knocked on a woman's door. She said she only read Proust, Kafka, and Šalamun.

"I am Šalamun," he said.

And critics call his life's work absurdist.

A "Difficult" Poet

What is the context for all this? When Tomaž Šalamun was born in 1941, his native Yugoslavia was invaded by the Nazi-led Axis powers. His family, as the poet made a point to often repeat in interviews, was persecuted by fascists and "suffered through two wars, fascism, communism—the center of Europe was really crushed."[2] During the poet's lifetime, Yugoslavia underwent a series of terrifying political crises: the decades-long Presidency-for-Life of the dictator Tito, the 1980s economic downturns, and ethnic conflicts of enormous scale, culminating in the Balkan Wars and the breakup of Yugoslavia.

---

1. Nester *The Critical Flame*
2. Nester *The Critical Flame*

Imagine a world in which pronouncing the word "bread" in the wrong accent could get you killed. Imagine watching the very name of your birthplace, the Balkan region, become a term for political explosion. From 1993 on, the International Criminal Tribunal for the former Yugoslavia tried political and military leaders from the region for war crimes and genocide: these trials continued through Tomaž Šalamun's life and for years after his death.

Critics label Šalamun a "difficult poet," a "fragmented poet," an absurdist, a surrealist—but this "difficulty" of style happened during a moment of extreme historical, social, and political difficulty. I would argue that the fragmentation of his poetry reflects the fragmentation of his homeland, perhaps even the fragmentation of the identity of everyone within that country. The point here is not to say that every absurdist must be standing in front of a burning building. The point is to say: We must open our eyes to see if there is in fact a building on fire behind the absurdist reading his verses. If so, might there be a whole other level of meaning we are missing?

"My chaotic background," Šalamun said, "shows in my language."[3]

Let's consider Šalamun's language: I open this book to any page and see tonal vitality, as if a child were playing with nouns instead of found objects. The pages are so filled with exclamations and fresh turns of phrase that one senses a kind of alluring arbitrariness, as if one were tapping into an energy source that no one knew existed, driven by vocabulary instead of combustion. That energy doesn't only fly off the page, it produces pages. I have heard different numbers cited as to how many books Šalamun has published. Some say forty-eight, others forty-nine. Brian Henry says he published fifty-two individual collections—but what's a book or two or three between friends?

The author and the text still need a reader, and Šalamun was rarely shy about addressing his own readers, whether on the subject of how he should be read, or indeed how he felt about readers in general:

> Whoever reads me
> as ironic
> will be guilty
>
> before God.
> I don't care about

---

3. Nester *The Critical Flame*

> your decadent
> defense systems,
> all this embossed
> criminal shit
>
> you proclaim
> to be humor and
> the cornerstone
>
> of your
> historical
> experience.

About the reader, he says:

> like a loyal devoted
> dog, I lick your
> golden head,
> reader.

How's that for poetic difficulty?

His Dualities

About Tomaž Šalamun, Tomaž Šalamun says:

> Tomaž Šalamun is a monster.
> Tomaž Šalamun is a sphere rushing in the air.
> No one knows his orbit.
> He lies down in twilight, he floats in twilight.
> The people and I look at him, astonished.

It might be useful to dwell for a moment on the idea of monstrosity here.

One aspect of this work that might be especially useful for the American readers in the second decade of the twenty-first century is this poet's perspective on how a protest poem might function, or rather on what indeed a protest poem, or a literary subversion, is:

When I came out of jail, people from the Secret Service—the UDBA—said, "Oh, you lost your steam, you don't write any protest poems anymore." My second book, still published by myself, was about butterflies, about nothing. It was more subversive than if I had written protest poems, since the government needed to show its pluralism and democracy. One has to be very precise not to be corrupt or used. I was fighting to be free within my writing. And just this was subversive, and therefore political.[4]

In our time when lack of nuance is apparent and a slogan of "who isn't with us is against us" appears on *all* sides of the political divide, Šalamun's experience seems, to me, priceless.

What I love about Brian Henry's monumental work of lucidly translating and selecting the poems for this book is the marvelous variation between the direct voice of poems such as these above—and some more rhapsodic poems and other more dreamlike narratives about his family and friends. I am also quite moved by the eerie feeling of premonition, which appears in later, previously untranslated work. "Clarity is our deepest mystery," Mahmoud Darwish is reported to have said. This comes across very strongly in Šalamun's late poetry, whose images are as strange as they are perfectly, strangely clear:

My small bones love
your small bones.

A tremendous feeling.
Flowers grow above us.

People stomp.
Some have wet shoes.

They light candles and smack their lips.
They're attractive. Our

small bones—entire little owls.
If you dig them out of

---

4. Simic *Bomb Magazine*

the ground, they frighten
no one. They're sacred

bones. Ossa sacra,
mamma mia.

The poet in these lines speaks as if from the underworld, as if he already knows his funeral will happen on a sunny day in Ljubljana, and there will be 300 poets in attendance—and he is speaking directly to them. Yet his voice doesn't cease the strange, sometimes vivid, at other times comedic, wonderment. Despite—or because of—all the comedy, surrealism, and absurdity, his main project is the ongoingness of awe. This curious duality is at the core of this poet's work. There is a surrealist, absurdist, ecstatic outburst, yes, but there are also moments of prolonged quiet that attain a magnetic quality. Reading these late poems, I can't seem to forget Tomaž's long silence during the Balkan Wars, and how there was something both political and spiritual about it. In retrospect, this duality feels very magnetic:

> During the Balkan Wars, when Brodsky and Miłosz were able to write something, I was completely silent. I didn't write a line of anything from 1989 to 1994. I just stopped writing. I think if you did intend to show that anger or depression, you wouldn't be able to write good poetry. But just being what you are, to be free within your writing, this is also the center of the real responsibility of the world. Therefore, your freedom is a political act.[5]

His Influences

Šalamun's influences are well buried. The poets he always praises are not necessarily the poets he borrows from. Here is one of his most famous lyrics:

> This is Tomaž Šalamun, he went to the store
> with his wife Maruska to buy milk
> so that he'd have milk to drink.
> And this is history.

---

5. Mort *Something Indecent*

One might hear here the echo of Šalamun's beloved Velimir Khlebnikov: "I need but little! A cup of milk, / a crust of bread. The sky. / And, over-head, these clouds!"[6] But I am more inclined to hear the direct link with Yehuda Amichai: "A man all alone in a room / practices on a drum, that too is history."[7]

Or, take this lyric which Tomaž once told me was influenced by John Ashbery:

The history
of heaven's growth
is the movement

of every eyelash
on every
born and unborn

human face . . .

Every pain
of every trembling
of the earth is

every cry
of all the children set down
at birth

Yes, one might compare the above to Ashbery of *Three Poems*, which Šalamun often mentioned to his friends, but I sense a direct link to William Blake:

I wander thro' each charter'd street,
Near where the charter'd Thames does flow.
And mark in every face I meet
Marks of weakness, marks of woe.

---

6. Khlebnikhov *Collected Works*
7. Amichai 156

In every cry of every Man,
In every Infants cry of fear,
In every voice: in every ban,
The mind-forg'd manacles I hear[8]

Having said that, I sense that the best commenter on Šalamun's process is Šalamun himself: "All my / thinking / is // technical. / Like the thinking / of trees."

Many Šalamuns

Šalamun's is a kind of writing that "makes many strange and inscrutable observations," as Irishman Colm Tóibín suggested in *The Guardian*, a kind of writing that "makes you sit up and not think, which is perhaps the real point of poetry."

Perhaps. The most convincing criticism of this work seems to come from Slovenian literary critic Miklavž Komelj, who, while praising Šalamun's inventiveness in *Transom*, hastens to note that "in this dynamism there is also a monotone quality, which the poet makes no attempt to hide. It is as if this ecstasy resulted from spinning endlessly in a circle, like the whirling dervishes—a religious order, incidentally, that was founded by the mystic Rumi, one of Šalamun's favorite poets. It seems that the intensity of Šalamun's language," Komelj concluded, "lies precisely in the endless insistence of its pulsation."

Perhaps. To my mind, it would be imprudent to make broad critical gestures in relation to a body of work that has enormous tonal range and spans thousands of pages.

There are, to put it simply, many Šalamuns. Sometimes, reading his poems, I get a sense Tomaž is like a spiritual seeker walking through the rubble of disbelief, searching, with his flashlight for a fellow human being, and unable to find one.

Finally, he begins to sing to himself, while looking, and he is looking so much, and can't find anyone, but he never stops looking.

And then he finds one! And then he is screaming again from ecstasy because he's found a dozen! But they are all Tomaž Šalamun.

My Šalamun is a poet of light touch, as spiritual as he is playful, a poet

---

8. Blake *Poems of William Blake*

whose sense of humor is combined with the surreal in a way not unlike (to my own surprise) these lines from Wallace Stevens:

> Remus, blow your horn!
> I'm ploughing on Sunday,
> Ploughing North America.
> Blow your horn![9]

I can't recall if it was 2005 or 2006 when I visited Tomaž in Pittsburgh, but I know it was the end of the semester, and as always Tomaž was surrounded by a small crowd of adoring young poets. Most of them were extremely comfortable with him—he was a master of finding the correct tone with many very different people.

As the poet was talking about packing his things to go back to Slovenia, one student made an offhand compliment on how after he left, the university should put a plaque on the door saying that a great poet lived here.

"When I leave they will indeed put a sign—" Tomaž thoughtfully said, then smiled. "It will say that the room is available for rent."

After Tomaž died, many essays remembering him were published, one after another, all of them focusing on the over-the-top tonalities of his work. That confuses the man and the speaker of his poems, I feel. The speaker in his lyrics enjoys extremities of tone, yes. But the man I remember was once asked at a party what was the most important thing human beings tend to ignore.

There was a brief quiet in the conversation. Then Tomaž chuckled.

"Modesty," he said.

Echo

On some days I wonder if Šalamun's absurdism is in fact a rather realistic portrayal of a postmodern, hypermediated world where we witness and are often terrified of our species's power. In this society where a modern person is shocked into the realization that, intellectually, one has very little room to dream anymore, a response such as Šalamun's is actually quite logical—maybe even the only sane response. He is reaching for the extremes because, in this dry period, a human being (as human beings always do) is longing for the ecstatic moment.

---

9. Stevens *Collected Poems*

Tomaž Šalamun is a postmodern poet, yes, but there is also an echo of something shamanistic, ancient, and raw in his writings.

Human beings have lived on the land now known as Slovenia for over 250,000 years. A pierced cave bear-bone flute, dating from approximately 43100 BP, was found there in 1995. It's quite possibly the oldest musical instrument discovered in the world.

All these years later, we still long for music.

ILYA KAMINSKY

Sources

Amichai, Yehuda. *The Selected Poetry Of Yehuda Amichai*. Translated by Chana Bloch and Stephen Mitchell. Los Angeles: University of California Press, 2013: 156.

Blake, William. *Poems of William Blake*. Project Gutenberg, 1996. https://www.gutenberg.org/ebooks/574.

Khlebnikhov, Velemir. *Collected Works*. Moscow: Gorky Institute of World Literature, 2006.

Mort, Valzhyna, ed. *Something Indecent: Poems Recommended by Eastern European Poets*. Pasadena: Red Hen Press, 2013.

Nester, Daniel. Interview with Tomaž Šalamun. The Critical Flame 60 (September 2019): http://criticalflame.org/conversations-tomaz-salamun-and-daniel-nester/.

Simic, Charles and Tomaž Šalamun. Conversation. Bomb Magazine (September 20, 2008): https://bombmagazine.org/articles/charles-simic-and-tomaž-šalamun/.

Stevens, Wallace. *Wallace Stevens: Collected Poetry and Prose*. New York: Library of America, 1997.

Tóibín, Colm. "The comet's trail." *The Guardian*, May 28, 2004. https://www.theguardian.com/books/2004/may/29/featuresreviews.guardianreview33.

Transom. Interview with Miklavž Komelj. *Transom 3* (Spring 2012). https://www.transomjournal.com/s/Transom-Issue-3.pdf.

INTRODUCTION

The Poet

"To become a poet is to step into the void, to jump into the dark."[1]

Born in Zagreb on July 4, 1941, Tomaž Šalamun grew up in Koper, a seaside town near Trieste, Italy, that became part of Yugoslavia after World War II. Because of his father's political difficulties with the Communist regime, his family moved around for several years, eventually settling in Koper. Šalamun has said, "What really defines me, basically, is that I grew up on the border between two worlds in the Cold War," and he has described his "background" as "very, very chaotic," "the result of the terrible history of 20th century Central Europe," which he believed "shows in [his] language."[2]

Šalamun started writing poetry at the age of twenty-two after seeing the Slovenian poet Dane Zajc (1929–2005) give a reading. To him, Zajc "had such a magical presence, an angel jumped out of his shoulders."[3] Šalamun recalled that his "first five poems came in half an hour, and felt like stones falling from the sky."[4] After he had written just twenty poems, he was elected editor of the subversive literary journal *Perspektive*, which, along with his poem "Duma 1964" (see Appendix), led to his arrest. He was told that he'd spend twelve years in prison, but due to international pressure, was released from prison after only five days. He emerged as a cultural celebrity, which made him feel compelled to write more poems in order to live up to his newfound notoriety. Although free from prison, he was still locked out of mainstream publishing in Yugoslavia, so his first two books—*Poker* (1966) and *The Purpose of a Cloak* (1968)—were published in samizdat. Despite an enthusiastic reception in some quarters, Šalamun's poetry was seen as a threat to the status quo. The Slovenian poet and playwright Ivo Svetina has written about how Šalamun "desacralized" and shunned "proper, high, literary use" of the language,[5] which led to a "chorus" of voices in Slovenia that "shouted about the danger that comes with Šalamun's poetry, almost a natural disaster that will topple both the foundations and superstructure of society, both the community of the nation and the basic cell of society, both matter and spirit, both language

1. Henry 186
2. Nester *The Critical Flame*
3. Henry 185
4. Hawkey 333
5. Svetina 906

and literature."[6] Šalamun was also prohibited stable employment and had to resort to piecemeal work such as selling encyclopedias door to door, translating nonliterary texts, and smuggling jewelry from Italy into Yugoslavia.

Šalamun studied art history, as well as history and architecture, at the University of Ljubljana, later becoming a curator and a founding member of the conceptual art group OHO, which took him to the United States for the first time in 1970 as part of an exhibit at the Museum of Modern Art. He credited his month in New York with changing his life because it turned his attention toward American culture. That connection was further strengthened two years later when he returned to North America as a guest of the International Writing Program at the University of Iowa, which led to two chapbooks in English translation: *Turbines* (1973) and *Snow* (1974). Šalamun has said that spending so much time in the United States and being away from Slovenia were essential to his growth as a poet, in part because (according to Slovenian poet and art historian Miklavž Komelj) he "always needed immense spaces; not only transoceanic and intercontinental distances, but intergalactic. And interlingual."[7]

Because of political difficulties in Yugoslavia, Šalamun could not return to the United States for a few years, and another collection in English translation would not appear until 1988, when Charles Simic edited a volume of Šalamun's selected poems for Ecco (Simic also translated many of the poems in the book, using Serbian translations of the Slovenian poems). In a 2008 conversation with Simic, Šalamun said, "I was fighting to be free within my writing. And just *this* was subversive, and therefore political. . . . The really bad years were the mid-'70s. . . . Coming back from America, from Iowa in 1973, I was annihilated. I couldn't make any money."[8] Still, Šalamun felt that it was "vital to be free in the language" despite the political situation in Yugoslavia at the time.[9] For him, poetry "participates in and is part of a tower that is five thousand years old and that has built-in instincts . . . for freedom."[10]

The Slovenian art historian Tomaž Brejc has discussed how Šalamun's urge to leave "the tribe" allowed him to "see better," to "examine history, the nation's essence and its current pulse," and to "introduce an international language" into Slovenia.[11] As a result, Šalamun "created a paradigm

---

6. Svetina 904

7. Komelj *Primorske Novic*

8. Simic *Bomb Magazine*

9. Šteger 579

10. Šteger 580

11. Brejc 951

of an open, polyglot life for Slovenes in this century, a skillfully moving subject who changes languages like changing planes and taxis, newspapers and encyclopedias, money and messages."[12] In a review of the 1988 *Selected Poems*, the Slovenian poet and cultural critic Aleš Debeljak (1961–2016) wrote that Šalamun never seemed "squarely integrated into the Slovene paradigm" mainly because of "his unrestricted and forceful desire always to be already somewhere else—moving through the past and the present, traversing the many different vocabularies and strange provinces of the mind and geography, always on the go."[13] Nevertheless, Debeljak claims, Šalamun "single-handedly changed the course of Slovene literature . . . balancing the cosmopolitan sensibility and persistent Slovene obsession with its precarious cultural position of being squeezed between two major cultures, Italian and German."[14] From the 1980s until shortly before his death in 2014, Šalamun was a frequent visitor to the United States: he was a Fulbright Scholar in New York in 1986, the Cultural Attaché for the Slovenian Embassy in New York in the late 1990s, and a visiting professor at numerous universities.

In addition to revolutionizing Slovenian literature, Šalamun has inspired several generations of poets from around the world. According to Brejc, Šalamun's poems are "above all large windows, fields of freedom for a new, direct perspective on words" that "initiated a great social liberation of language."[15] Komelj has explained how this liberation also extended to the political sphere, as Šalamun's commitment to total freedom in his poetry, including its open expressions of homosexual desire, "demanded a different mental climate" and "irreversibly changed the entire [Slovenian] space on all levels. For example: [Slovenian writer and lesbian activist] Nataša Velikonja can accurately cite his liberating poetry as one of 'the foundations on which gay and lesbian activism was formed in the mid 1980s'" in Slovenia.[16]

Šalamun mostly wrote early in the morning or in the middle of the night when a poem would awaken him. Remarkably prolific, he published fifty-two individual collections of poetry, fifteen of them between 1971 and 1981. And in the last decade of his life, he wrote twenty books, nine of which were published after his death. His one dry spell was in the early 1990s, when a personal crisis and the wars in the Balkans rendered him silent and "afraid of

---

12. Brejc 954
13. Debeljak 115
14. Debeljak 116
15. Brejc 953
16. Komelj *Primorske Novice*

poetry":[17] "God can crush you, if you, as I do with language, try to reach the borders of everything possible, the borders of language, to go to total transgression, to go to total blasphemy. . . . It was as if God took everything out of me, it was as if my head would explode, as if my brain would melt, and I was left in a completely dark, cold place, in total terror and feeling guilty and not being able to help myself, and I was not able to write for four and a half years after this happened to me."[18] Although the wars weighed heavily on him, he largely blamed himself for this silent period: "I'm constantly escaping God, quarreling with Him, and making terrible gestures, terrible blasphemies. I'm a cannibal against God, sometimes, and still I'm crushed in total humility."[19]

This tension, though, was usually productive for his poetry. Komelj has described how Šalamun "constantly moved in the realm of dreams and twilight, and knew that true existential freedom involves a confrontation with the monstrous."[20] In interviews, Šalamun has compared writing poetry to "religious delirium" because of its "intensity of delight and the feeling of something I don't understand that is deep, that regenerates me and also horrifies me,"[21] while also divulging that "writing is a total joy . . . a dance, an opening up, a standing and taking in of light, total delight": "I love the extremes. . . . I like to experience the utmost borders of sanity, to test my courage, then try to come back and still, in some gentle way, to expose myself to the most extreme dangers . . . [t]o increase the human experience."[22]

The Poetry

"Poetry has to be completely open . . . it has to discover spaces which were not discovered."[23]

Šalamun is everywhere and nowhere in his poems. In a foreword to a second edition of Poker (1989), Tomaž Brejc describes how Šalamun's poems engage in "constant movement": "social, verbal, physical mobility, the mobility of history, capital, political categories, fate, movements through time, and people who move from history to the present of a memory or repeated

---

17. Henry 184
18. Henry 186–187
19. Henry 187
20. Komelj *Primorske Novice*
21. Šteger 551
22. Nester *The Critical Flame*
23. Young 106

experience, encounter."[24] Past and present often overlap in his work, which employs "synchronous and simultaneous projection."[25] The ostensible setting of a Šalamun poem can change at any point, as can the verb tense. Pronouns might or might not have clear antecedents. He bends time, space, and syntax, undoing conventional understandings of how things—images, ideas, memories, dreams, reveries, actions, people, objects, animals—can connect. The fabric of Šalamun's poetry is extraordinarily variegated. In addition to friends, family, and other poets, his poems reference numerous visual artists, filmmakers, composers, philosophers, and various political and military figures throughout history. Šalamun's poems offer an unpredictable mixture of high lyricism, slang, autobiography, narrative, history, politics, surrealism, absurdity, camp, mysticism, grandeur, and self-mythology. The self-mythologizing in his poems is both ironic and self-aware—a way of dealing with the historical and political realities of Yugoslavia at the time.

Perhaps unsurprisingly considering his background, Šalamun's early influences are international and wide-ranging: Rumi, William Blake, Walt Whitman, Comte de Lautréamont, Arthur Rimbaud, Oton Župančič, William Carlos Williams, T. S. Eliot, Velimir Khlebnikov, Osip Mandelstam, Vladimir Mayakovsky, Henri Michaux, Edvard Kocbek, Vasko Popa, Allen Ginsberg, Frank O'Hara, and John Ashbery (particularly *Three Poems*). Sometimes he read these poets in their original languages, but he also read many of the non-Slovenian poets in Croatian, Italian, Serbian, and Slovenian translation (for example, while he read Eliot in Slovenian, he read Williams in Italian). His work also has affinities with poets associated with Language poetry and the second generation of the New York School, including Ted Berrigan, Clark Coolidge, and Bob Perelman. And throughout his life Šalamun continued to read and feel energized by poetry from around the world, especially the United States and Slovenia.

One of Šalamun's goals in his poetry was to enliven language. For poetry, what mattered most to him was "how in the center you are, how you are able to be there where you are needed to be, in the heat of the language."[26] According to Brejc, a Šalamun poem is "a surface, a weaving, a cellular structure, a network, a fragment of a teleological covering of words in time and space, valid ahead of time and in retrospect, for any location. There is no lacuna anywhere, no lapse that would uncover a clumsy, uninventive use of

24. Brejc 941–942
25. Brejc 947
26. Henry 188

words, it's all an attempt to have the creative experience completely provided by a controlled fantasy drive, with cascades of intuition, protected for that moment when the poem can happen."[27] Brejc also notes that "the physicality of Šalamun's speech is oriented toward the resurrection of words."[28] This focus on revivifying language only intensified as Šalamun grew older. The Slovenian poet Miha Maurič has written about how Šalamun approached the language of poetry as "a destroyer of both spatial and temporal dimensions"[29] and about how his later poetry "creates a world where grammatical rules are annihilated and reconfigured anew."[30] Šalamun viewed his poetic process as mostly intuitive, with his poems emerging "from a certain place that isn't a place that I control, but has a certain autonomy and also authority of its own."[31] Maurič has said that Šalamun compared his creative process to "conducting an electric current."[32] And Šalamun told one of his translators that he "does not know what all this language is, where it comes from, or what it means. He only knows that *it is*, and that it is his nature to work with it, destroy it, reassemble it . . ."[33]

Over time, Šalamun honed the ability to skim the surface of the mind (images, memories, impressions) while exploring the depths (myth, folklore, history, visual art, literature, film). His poems are full of surprises and paradoxes, thrumming with tenderness and terror, absurdity and awe, audacity and humility, the familiar and the surreal. In the space of a few lines, he can veer from astonishing insight to utter silliness. The speaker of his poems is both a sage and a jester, both a prophet and an "oaf." Above all, he is a figure in a constant state of wonder.

Šalamun's poems incorporate words and phrases from numerous languages as well as regional Slovenian and Istrian dialects. This openness to other languages allows him to introduce sounds, connections, and statements not found in his native language. In addition to "foreign" words and phrases, his poems are brimming with names, locations, and sometimes invented words, technical language or jargon (e.g., nautical terms that he learned as a boy). The range of his vocabulary and references is

---

27. Brejc 945
28. Brejc 949
29. Maurič 534
30. Maurič 539
31. Koršič *LUD Literatura*
32. Maurič 538
33. Young xviii

staggering.[34] Brejc offers a useful primer for reading Šalamun's poetry: "the eye must glide along the surface of the poem and quickly connect meanings, ideas" while reckoning with "the most varied knowledge . . . , different languages and dialects, names and facts, from the most general, lexical, encyclopedic to those that only a family doctor has . . ."[35]

Šalamun's freewheeling autobiographical poems are reminiscent of Frank O'Hara, but can be more harrowing, particularly those written while he was torn between marrying Metka Krašovec (his second wife) and remaining with his lover (Alejandro Gallegos Duval) in Mexico, a dilemma that animates his book *Ballad for Metka Krašovec* (1981). And like O'Hara, he often refers to friends in his poems, usually by first name and with no context, alongside historical and cultural figures, some prominent, many obscure or local, making no distinctions among them. But few of his poems focus solely on his personal life, instead expanding outward (in space) and backward (in time) to engage the larger world beyond the self.

While the forms of Šalamun's poetry vary, he wrote predominantly in stanzaless free verse, quatrains, tercets, and couplets, which are ubiquitous in his later work. Many of his poems are in a form that he called a "sonnetoid": a fourteen-line poem that inhabits the lyric space of the sonnet without following the form's conventions. His sonnetoids are mainly composed of two quatrains and two tercets, a single fourteen-line block of text, or, in his final years, seven couplets.

Although Šalamun did not write critical prose, he shed light on his poetics in interviews, as when he said that writing poetry can be "diabolical, because it cuts things apart, it goes very deep and makes space and touches places we probably should not touch. But the diabolic position does not come from dark, it comes from light, from wanting to bring light as far as it can go. Sometimes the language is very happy and it does things like a dolphin, it is pure grace, you just follow grace, and you have this feeling of water and light. The dolphin is the language. You don't know what it is. It's important that you don't lose faith in going toward it. I have enough faith to just jump, to be a part of it, to go with it. . . . Language takes you

---

34. In a linguistic analysis of Šalamun's *When: Selected Poems* (2011), Vesna Mikolič notes that 6,187 words (56% of the words in the 900-page book) appear only once, which "confirms the poet's intention to create his own world with language." She posits that "the exceptional richness of Šalamun's lexicon" is the result of both an enormous vocabulary and his proclivity for neologisms, "vulgarisms," slang, colloquialisms, regional dialects, and foreign words.

35. Brejc 947

forward, and you endure it as long as you can endure."[36] And near the end of his life, he said, "wherever the path of language leads me, I'm always aware that I am a healer of language. . . . For me, the healing position of my own trauma begins where the wound is most direct, where it glows the most. In the glow, in the deepest darkness, there is the most light."[37]

The Selection

Šalamun's books in English include three volumes of selected poems published between 1988 and 1997, five miscellaneous compilations published between 2000 and 2015, and ten individual books published between 2001 and 2022. There has been no comprehensive volume of selected poems since *The Four Questions of Melancholy: New and Selected Poems* (1997), which covers twenty-five of his first twenty-six books. My primary aims for editing *Kiss the Eyes of Peace: Selected Poems 1964–2014* are to gather in a single volume Šalamun's best poems from his five decades of writing, to affirm his place as a world poet, to convey the full scope of his writing life, and to showcase his artistic range as well as his dominant poetic concerns and obsessions.

An important reference point for this book is Šalamun's own volume of selected poems in Slovenian, *Kdaj* (*When*), published in 2011. Over 900 pages long, the book includes poems from forty-one of his books, along with some previously uncollected poems from the 1960s and some new poems that later appeared in different books in Slovenia. My editorial process began with *Kdaj*, with the poems that Šalamun himself had chosen. Then I went through all fifty-two of his individual books, making preliminary translations of each poem to decide which poems to translate fully. I looked for poems that would enrich or expand the prevailing perceptions of Šalamun's poetry, add something new (thematically or formally) to his oeuvre in English, and/or contribute something new to English-language poetry in general. I was particularly interested in poems that had not been translated into English before, and many of the poems in this book (around 45% of the total) are appearing in English for the first time. I also gave extra attention to major books that have not been translated into English yet: *Pilgrimage for Maruška* (1971), *White Ithaka* (1972), *Arena* (1973), and *The Voice* (1983). I eventually translated twelve to fifteen poems from all fifty-two books, which produced a collection of 700 poems that I

---

36. Young 104–105
37. Šteger 558

gradually narrowed to 240 poems. I selected at least one poem from each of his books, as well as the early uncollected poem "Duma 1964" and two unpublished poems written at the very end of his life.

The Translations

> "I don't see a problem if there's a lot of ambiguity. . . . Some
> sentences walk in the mist, some bend strangely, I like
> awkwardness, awkwardness is the crucial thing in my writing.
> Things should not be clear. If clear they're too domesticated.
> I dedomesticate, invade the language, delogify. . . . I function
> through paradox, negativity, opposites."[38]

When translating Šalamun's poetry, I try to strike a balance between being both accurate and literal (which in his case generally means avoiding overinterpretation, smoothing out rough patches, clarifying intentional ambiguities, and resolving paradoxes) and producing a poem in English that carries over various stylistic aspects of the original. Šalamun preferred literal translations of his poems, but he also welcomed the new possibilities— of expression, juxtaposition, music—afforded by translation. The risk of entirely literal translations of poems is that they can seem more like artifacts than poems—what Paul Valéry called "anatomical specimens."[39] The opposite side of that risk is the translator imposing their own poetics on what they're translating, pulling the translated text too far from the original and producing something that seems more like imitation than translation. I want my translations to function as poems in English while not necessarily appearing to have been written in English: ideally, they are adjacent primary texts that depend on, and are imbued with the style of, the original but also stand on their own. As a poet myself, I pay as much attention to sound as to meaning, which seems especially relevant for Šalamun poems that carry an unsettling, discordant, or spell-like music.

Because Šalamun's work can be baffling even to native Slovenian speakers, I have kept in mind John Keats's notion of negative capability—the ability to dwell in "uncertainties, Mysteries, doubts, without any irritable reaching after fact and reason"—while translating. This has helped me embrace ambiguity and resist the temptation to try to make more sense

---

38. Tomaž Šalamun, email to Brian Henry, July 24, 2006
39. Valéry 298

than there is in the original, to paraphrase difficult passages, or to untangle purposely thorny phrases. Because of their syntax, internal movement, range of references, use of different dictions and tones, and multilingualism, Šalamun's poems are often elusive in the original, so they should not become overly accessible during the process of translation.

Of course, a certain level of interpretation is necessary for translation, not least when deciding which meaning of a word to use. For example, the title of the poem "Milost" from *Poker* can be translated as "Mercy," "Pity," or "Grace," and different translators will choose different options based on their interpretation of the poem. The Slovenian word "vrata" can mean "door" or "gate," "roka" can be a hand or an arm, and "zemlja" can mean "earth," "ground," "land," or "soil." The translator must figure out which to use, even when the context remains unclear. And because Slovenian does not use articles before nouns, the translator must determine whether or not "the" or "a(n)" should go before a noun, which also requires interpretation.

Though written in Slovenian, Šalamun's poems include words, phrases, and entire passages in Croatian, English, French, German, Italian, and Spanish as well as regional dialects. Early in the process of translating the poems in this book, I distinguished text translated from a language other than Slovenian (as well as text already in English) by italicizing it. I became dissatisfied with this approach because Šalamun himself sometimes used italics for emphasis, so the newly italicized text added emphasis not present in the original poems. And using italics in two different ways seemed out of sync with Šalamun's polylingual poetics. He moved fluidly among many languages, so the shift from Slovenian to French, for example, would not seem unusual or even noteworthy to him, but italicizing a phrase translated from a language other than Slovenian would call additional attention to it. I also considered leaving all the non-Slovenian text in its original language, but the potential barrier to comprehension for English readers would conflict with the seamlessness of Šalamun's movement among different languages. When non-Slovenian, non-English text can be easily understood or translated by English readers (e.g., "mamma mia," "Gastarbeiter," "mon amour fou"), I left it in the original language. I ultimately decided to format the text translated from other languages the same way as the text translated from Slovenian, using italics only when Šalamun did.

For titles, I adhered to the examples of the poems' appearances in their original books, not to English translations that added titles to untitled poems. Šalamun's relationship to poem titles can be difficult to pin down, especially with his earlier work. Some poems that were untitled upon initial publication received titles in his 1980 volume of selected poems but were again untitled in the 2011 selected poems. I deviated from the original books only when a later appearance in a Slovenian book used a title that seemed illuminating or intriguing. If a poem was never given a title in any of its Slovenian appearances, I generally refrained from adding one, even if the poem had been given a title in another English translation.

If a poem does not contain punctuation in the original, I did not add punctuation; and if a poem uses unconventional punctuation (such as commas where periods or semicolons ordinarily would be used), I carried that over into the translation. I typically retained Slavic names and Šalamun's stanza structures and his approach to capitalization (or lack thereof). Many of Šalamun's poems employ severe enjambment, breaking lines in the middle of prepositional phrases, predicates (including reflexive verbs), and similes, in part because he considered the beginning of lines to be as meaningful as the endings of lines. My translations follow his approach to enjambment, even when differences in Slovenian and English syntax required reconfiguring the relationship between a sentence and a line. The end result, I hope, is a compelling poem in English that maintains the key stylistic elements of the original.

After reading Šalamun's early poems in Slovenian, I noticed that many of them had been translated rather loosely—lines had been cut, stanzas added or reconfigured, titles added to untitled poems, names anglicized—perhaps in an effort to make the work more palatable to American readers. Indeed, some of his best-loved poems in English translation appear to be the products of domestication, which might have been helpful in introducing a Slovenian poet to American readers in the 1970s and 1980s. Now, with eighteen books published in English, Šalamun's work should need no such interventions. So I have followed the original poems as closely as possible, even if that means deviating from previous translations.

One of the most challenging parts of translating the poems in this book was making new translations of my favorite poems, some of which are well known in their earlier English versions. After my publisher asked me to translate every poem in this book rather than use existing translations, I took some solace in the fact that even Šalamun retranslated some of his own poems, always with notably different results, reinforcing the idea that great poems can stand up to many translations, especially over time. In a few cases, a new translation provides an opportunity to fix significant problems with an earlier translation, as when an earlier translation strayed too far from the original, dropping lines (e.g., two lines in "Sand," seven lines in "History," over twenty lines in "Painted Desert") or changing the order of lines (as in "History") or the number or structure of stanzas. In other cases, a new translation can move the poem in English closer to the original and unravel some of the domestication that was fairly common with the early translations. And in every case, a new translation can offer a different angle, interpretation, sonic scaffolding, and/or emphasis, unlocking or highlighting new aspects of the poem.

An example: one of Šalamun's most famous lines in English (from his poem "Tree of Life") is "I was born in a wheat field snapping my fingers." The original line reads "Rodil sem se v žitu in tleskal s prsti." The word "žito" means grain or cereal, not wheat, which would be "pšenica." The Slovenian word "in" means "and," so the narrator is saying that he was born and then snapped his fingers. The image of the poet being born snapping his fingers is one of ultimate coolness. The image of the poet being born and then snapping his fingers is one of almost divine power, which seems more consistent with Šalamun's view of the power of poetry. "I was born in a field of grain and snapped my fingers" thus seems more faithful both to the meaning of the original and to Šalamun's poetics.

While poetry generally relies on repetition, Šalamun had a roster of words that he repeated—both within poems and across poems—as touchstones. One of my priorities in translating so many of his poems was to preserve the original repetition as much as possible, rather than using synonyms within poems or in different poems. For example, variations on the word "strašen" (which means "terrible," "horrible," "frightful," etc.) appear over seventy-five times in his 2011 volume of selected poems, but the word has been translated in different ways over time, diminishing the power of repetition within and across poems. I decided on "terrible" because of the word's frequent spiritual undertone in his poems and direct connection to "terror." Having a single translator for all of these poems helps with consistency in translation choices. I also retranslated my own translations from 2006 to 2014 for the sake of consistency and accuracy.

The process of translating hundreds of Šalamun's poems written over a span of fifty years reinforced for me the fact that his poems, however seemingly random or driven by the subconscious, illuminate the connections between humanity and the natural world (including inanimate objects) in the past and in the present. As he became older, more and more of his poems declined to focus on a singular moment or idea and instead radiated outward physically, temporally, and mentally as if he were trying to embrace all of existence, with no demarcations or hierarchies. As if all were a continuum and everything (and everyone) were connected.

BRIAN HENRY

Sources

Brejc, Tomaž. "Tomaž Šalamun and Julian Schnabel." In Tomaž Šalamun's *Kdaj*, 939–954. My translation.

Debeljak, Aleš. Review of *Selected Poems*. *Slovene Studies* 12.1 (1990): 115–116.

Hawkey, Christian and Tomaž Šalamun. "A Correspondence." *Chicago Review* 52.2 (2006): 332–339.

Henry, Brian. Interview with Tomaž Šalamun. *Verse* 15.3/16.1 (1998): 179–189.

Komelj, Milkavž. "I was never a human. Always an angel." *Primorske Novice* (January 9, 2015): http://www.primorske.si/plus/7--val/-nikdar-nisem-bil -clovek--vedno-angel--. My translation.

Koršič, Petra. Interview with Tomaž Šalamun. *LUD Literatura* (May 13, 2015): https://www.ludliteratura.si/intervju/tomaz-salamun-dobra-poezija-siri -svet-pomaga-dihanju-zemlje-prinasa-lepoto-mir/. My translation.

Maurič, Miha. "In the Interior of Language." In Tomaž Šalamun's *Jutro*, 529– 540. My translation.

Mikolič, Vesna. "A Literary Perspective on Šalamun's Poetic Discourse Through Slovenian and Foreign-Language Lexicon." https://centerslo.si/wp-content /uploads/2015/10/33-Mikolic.pdf. My translation.

Nester, Daniel. Interview with Tomaž Šalamun. *The Critical Flame* 60 (September 2019): http://criticalflame.org/conversations-tomaz-salamun-and-daniel-nester/.

Simic, Charles and Tomaž Šalamun. Conversation. *Bomb Magazine* (September 20, 2008): https://bombmagazine.org/articles/charles-simic-and-tomaž-šalamun/.

Svetina, Ivo. "22. May 1965." In Tomaž Šalamun's *Kdaj*, 897–913. My translation.

Šteger, Aleš. "Vessel for Departure: A Conversation with Tomaž Šalamun." In Tomaž Šalamun's *Jutro*, 541–596. My translation.

Valéry, Paul. "Variations on the Eclogues." In *Collected Works*, Volume VII, 295– 312. Translated by Denise Folliot. Princeton: Princeton University Press, 1989.

Velikonja, Nataša. "Cracks in the heads of fascists." Delivered at the 25th Gay and Lesbian Film Festival, 2009. http://www.ljudmila.org/siqrd/fglf/25/razpoke .php. My translation.

Young, Jeffrey. "A Conversation with Tomaž Šalamun." *Trafika 5* (Autumn 1995): 104–107.

———. "Notes on the Translation." *Andes*, xi–xxii.

ECLIPSE (I)

I grew tired of the image of my tribe
and moved away

From long nails
I weld limbs for my new body.
From old rags, entrails.
A rotten coat of carrion
will be the coat of my solitude.
I pull my eye from the depths of the swamp.
From devoured plates of disgust
I will build a hut.

My world will be a world of sharp edges.
Cruel and everlasting.

ECLIPSE (II)

I'll take nails,
long nails
and drive them into my body.
Quite gently,
quite slowly,
so that it takes longer.
I'll make a detailed plan.
I'll upholster myself every day
for example some ten square centimeters.

Then I'll set fire to everything.
It'll burn a long time,
it'll burn for seven days.
Only the nails will remain,
soldered, all rusty.
So I'll remain.
So I'll survive everything.

PEACE TO THE PEOPLE ON EARTH

God remembers all travelers
                  the rain in Arras
            the son of David
  and a squirrel how it falls to the earth
    but I yell rabbits
  thinking they really are rabbits because I see poorly
    God remembers Stavrogin
stone pines decayed wood and our games
    how I pick my teeth
      and say peace to the people on earth
of all Empire-style furniture
    I like Empire-style legs the most
            God remembers
    God remembers how I tortured myself
      making a tetrahedron from bread
throwing it furiously at the wall
      and there was a war
      and the others ate saccharin
The fire gets closer
     night with whiskers
  I see hell where my angel stood

MERCY

About God very briefly
he never said abundance
never rosemary
never peaceful
and if there were ants in the corners
there were just ants in the corners

dust for example
where should it fall
down or sideways
or should there be roots
God solves all this insanely slowly

sometimes he says ARCHAIC
but no one stirs
no one wakes up
no one actually wakes up
sometimes he says we slaughtered the flower bearers
and buys bright paper
I bought bright paper he says
we slaughtered the flower bearers
and commands the little boat to float on the sea
the trees bow
but something falls so that it splashes

you are the light of the world
a city on a mountain cannot hide

RESPONSIBILITY

Have you already seen God
how he's rushing to arrive on time by two thirty
responsibility responsibility
you approach neither the beginning nor the end
immovable tethered
instead of swinging your legs like that
responsibility responsibility
a world without nature
a world without talking
trees are not responsible while they grow
and what does the word have to do with it
the sun doesn't need it when it sets
nor the sky which is only blue and nothing else
whom did God ask
when he created the butterfly the way it is
when he could have made its legs 15cm across
responsibility responsibility
baroque sustenance of the nation

HOMAGE TO A CAP UNCLE GUIDO AND ELIOT

Just like Cerar became a world champion
because something was wrong with his legs
I'll become an insanely great poet
because they disappointed me
with that blue cap from François
sent for Christmas 1946
so then I always had to
skip over him in our prayers
song of songs of the pan-Šalamunian religion
insanely democratic people's institution
because it contained everything
from stamps Cilka cookies Horak Kajfež
to that poor fool
who drank at his hotel in Ventimiglia
and wasted away in the world
like our prayer wasted away
its last major reformer was Uncle Guido
who was otherwise known among the people
because he invented a new pipe for steam boilers
but this wasn't his main profession
his main profession
was watering flowers
and just like Spinoza
only taller
he was constantly thinking about death
buying us ice cream
and every day rediscovering
what was between
the magnolia Brandenburg and America
two days ago Eliot died
my teacher

DRESS

what is your favorite color
my favorite color is yellow
would you wear a wig if your hair fell out overnight
if my hair fell out overnight I'd wear a wig
we were told you'd been in Portugal
could you briefly give us your impressions
Portugal is a small country
the people dress well
was it hot
it was hot in the sun
it was hot in the shade too
did you have an uncle with the air force
I had an uncle with the air force
did he influence you to decide on this profession
I wouldn't say he influenced
before long he died and then he didn't influence

SOLDIER

what is dearest to you in life
in life peace is dearest to me
would you follow a missionary
I think I would follow a missionary
but I'd still need to think it over
what has particularly upset you lately
I couldn't say what particularly upset me
do you feel the effects of the second world war
I do not feel the effects
I remember a soldier rushing at a gate
I remember seeing a blue butterfly
we ask that you communicate something to our listeners
very well I'm saying hello to Uncle Eugene who's now in Canada

WHERE IS NORTH, WHERE IS SOUTH

the first discovery speaks of the randomness of the world
the second discovery speaks of the precondition
the third discovery speaks of insinuating with the head
the fourth discovery speaks of a briefcase
the fifth discovery speaks of a method of distinction

I.
there are six lines on the wall
a convex edge in the corner
half a meter lower says Adelshoffen
on the left and right you can see a windowpane with iron trim that's
painted with minium

II.
all the northern countries are north of me
all the southern countries are south of me

III.
often it happens that I insinuate with my head

IV.
the first definition of a briefcase pushes the briefcase
the second definition of a briefcase pushes the briefcase
the third definition of a briefcase pushes the briefcase

V.
I produced the word *petaheva*
I produced the word *petaheva* again
as we distinguish a lizard from a lizard
so we also distinguish the first product from the second

BLUE

healers / flat sky / flame
gifts for the hill / dachshunds
blue cellophane / blue color of bread
blue white walls / dante
blood blue / outstretched wings blue
a terrible guardian angel protects maruška
blue kristof / semen blue / we'll die on the same day
blue enemies / tall blue figure
friends / we walk on the red sea blue / the scent of hay
ash / the world's end / blue delight
fairy tales and conjurers / flying over the coast
blue mouth / day / juice / boats
blue white ships / maria's messengers
blue karst / blue love / blue plains and body
use / blue wheat / speed / growth blue
light / buildings / blue shepherds and sailors
robbers / cobblers blue
blue foundations / blue storms / blue sand / breathing
blue face / crosses nailed to the wall
terrible blue mooing of an animal / earth / blue manhattan
good ripe fruit measured out by people
blue game / mountains / blue snow / sheep / machines
offerings / blue murder / yearning / dogs in the suburbs / money
blue jeans and prayers / women in markets / children
passion blue / grace / skin blue / silent blue rainbow
blessed sleep and words
blue light
blue day
blue fuck
blessed light / blue maruška / my wife

GABRIEL

dusk in summer?
mushrooms in summer.
it's sizzling in bohinj, a putto is blasting for dew

where in abundance?
there in abundance.
head bowed, a grave in the grain

what kind of narrative?
this kind of narrative.
the sea splashes, the first stem is sketched in the channel

where on the stone?
there on the stone.
baberle is dying, rue st. jacques

my command?
your command.
horses trot and stop before nighttime

when watteau?
now watteau.
we love grapes, on crampon tracks

who is porous?
he is porous.
beads roll, marinated sex

a bridge to the sky?
grain to the sky.
we fasten our seatbelts, smell gasoline

water from a rock?
salt from a rock.
listen to how it knits, how it wails, how it wakes

powder beneath the skis?
wind beneath the skis.
we exploit god's sun, sense wood

I HAVE A HORSE

I have a horse. The horse has four legs.
I have a turntable. On the turntable I sleep.
I have a brother. My brother is a sculptor.
I have a coat. I have a coat so that I'm not cold.
I have a plant. I have a plant so that there's greenery in the room.
I have Maruška. I have Maruška because I love her.
I have matches. With matches I light cigarettes.
I have a body. With a body I do the most beautiful things.
I have destruction. Destruction causes me a lot of problems.
I have night. Night comes to me through the window in the room.
I have a passion for car racing. From a passion for car racing I race cars.
I have money. With money I buy bread.
I have six truly good poems. I hope that I'll write even more.
I have lived twenty-seven years. All these years went by like lightning.
I have relatively a lot of courage. With this courage I fight against
    human stupidity.
I have a name day on March seventh. I'll be happy if March seventh is a
    nice day.
I have a little friend named Bredica. In the evening when they put her to
    bed she says Šalamun and falls asleep.

JONAH

how does the sun set?
like snow
what color is the sea?
wide
Jonah are you salty?
I'm salty
Jonah are you a flag?
I'm a flag
all the fireflies are resting

what are the stones like?
green
how do doggies play?
like the poppy
Jonah are you a fish?
I'm a fish
Jonah are you a sea urchin?
I'm a sea urchin
listen to the murmur

Jonah is the roe rushing through the forest
Jonah am I watching the mountain breathe
Jonah are all the houses
have you heard about the rainbow?
what is dew like?
are you asleep?

DRIVER

did you open his eyes? did you think he was hostile?
I didn't open his eyes. I didn't think he was hostile.
will you set him on fire? will you build him wings?
I won't set him on fire. I won't build him wings.
what is his profession?
chauffeur. he drives down dusty roads all day.
does he rush when it snows?
when it snows he puts on chains.
where did you meet him?
in the forest. he said he would be a pilot. he wondered
if it was much warmer in the south and if there was
a big difference in degrees.

ARE ANGELS GREEN?

are angels green? can heaven sustain them?
workers have a mouth, a face, a gait and children
little sheep lick the grass, tigers tear meat
water is always scooped up near the shore

I saw that a rainbow had fallen
shepherds swam over it
I waved, I waved, I felt myself burning
I knew I was awake, I didn't know who was singing

who made you, day? where do ants come from?
why does a thread stick together?
why does light fall on a knife?
foolish maturity, you scrub my collar

where are the blacksmiths to forge my horseshoes?
I don't like having my eyes covered
I want light to hit me, air
I want everyone to breathe, a mouse, shit

WHEN YOU CROSSED THE RIVER

when you crossed the river night fell
the hands are clean, I don't dare to look up
I don't dare to look at the water, death blazes
the fires are dark, the air is green dust

sometimes I pick a rose, it falls on your picture
you laugh, I sit on the pier
I hear oars, I hear wicked people
if only I could grow, if only I would spin

if only I would shine day and night, night and day
if only rain would fall, if only the light were terrible
if only I would look, touch and scream
if only the earth would open, if only the air were fresh

if only I could feel your skin, your teeth, your waist
if only I were yours, if only I could hold and caress you again
tell you fairy tales, breathe like you did
god, in order to speak, breathed, laughed like your shadow

GOD, HOW I GROW

god, how I grow
how strong I am, terrible and sly
how I undress, peel and move
this is your work, lord, I kill

in the garden there are flowers, air enters my mouth
in the desert there are butterflies, in mothers, meat
if I put a watch on my wrist, I cheer
drums, drums, steam flows, pours

blessed fuck, sovereign, your food is ours
peaches, bodies, mountains, smoke
the dead, their skin, necklaces
I pull out gold teeth, sell them for bread

angels rise from the sea, cherubim flutter
my verses are like splitting rocks
breaking jaws and screaming
may I eat my fill, god, be your law to the bottom

CHRISM

close the window, my genius cannot stand the air
silkworm flowers lick the chrome
light is censored status
darkness rides a horse, corrodes the trestle

all metals smell of color
I attach everything infantile to the edge
gold will never be next to gold
it will be covered by calm

o control, destructive fighters of advantage
winter lies in the mansion, a band of peacock ribbons
you can flash the searchlight
concealed in the tabernacle, knotted strand of a giant

equinox sunflower, the touch oozes
the berries are red, the phalanx knocks down the pyramid
the sea is repainted, steam splits
the swimmers are skating, history is impaled

THE RABBLE

all commands, all flowers are tepid
we'll have a bridge, a biscuit, a pond
a cold shower, a solidly shaped earth
tired dust, diluted crimea

in the south is petrinja, piles of wood
cracks for the smooth bread of beggars
a comely imperialist is breaking stars
the rabble has blotting paper on its belly

iron stretches and shrinks, rabid dogs
I know everything. the ontic plane is civilization.
sleep, don't name the trees
I know everything. the hills are a craft.

the planks are a concoction, the sword is free
I know everything. streets are terrible for innocence.
angels burn in hell and scratch the sand with their feet
the rabble has blotting paper on its belly

SARAJEVO

the passion of the rabble, the little furnace of the *logos*
the god of green rhymes, padded furs
the breast of a spring snake, the membranes of snails
hunger is blood, hunger is power
the colors of golden black skin
of dead guards, of the hands of lacquered drifters
car hoods, the killed glow of eros
smooth butterflies, sheets of his blood
he soothes far away, shines far away
walks nearby, devout pilgrims
a circle of grasses, the straightness of wood
the fires of meadows, the pasture's burden
how the mouth opened terribly
the berries of infernos, the luster of smoke offerings
the cube, the sheep stables
the wounded god, the sea of hair
the terrible transparency of white paper
the field of barking, smooth white boards
the son somehow rots, the soft skin of a roe
the water somehow flows, pineapple cartilage
hunters, the wedge between half-open windows
serene panes, pierced panes
the seven layers of troy, the burning of candles
the placing of sellotape, the falling of a thin string
the spinning of crumbs, heavy spheres suspended
ellipses, the angles of coiled wires
fatty fins, the axis of the sun and venus
the imaginary lines of body transfer
the grunting of airplanes, the cameramen of the ground
smooth-shaven animals, hot mess tins
mama among the tall grain, a shower beneath us
leaping with worn-out cardboard, the diagram on the pillars
calm down, fall in love and kill
calm down, imported beetle

WHO'S WHO

you are a genius tomaž šalamun
you are marvelous you are beautiful
you are tall you are a giant
you are powerful you are majestic
you are the greatest that ever lived
you are a king you are wealthy
you are a genius tomaž šalamun in accordance with nature we must admit
you are a lion the stars admire you
the sun turns to you every day
you are everything you are mount ararat
you are everlasting you are the morning star
you are without end and beginning you are without shadow and fear
you are the light you are heavenly fire
behold the eyes of tomaž šalamun behold the majestic light of heaven
behold his hands behold his waist
behold how he walks behold how he touches the ground
your skin smells of oil
your hair is solar dust
the stars marvel who marvels at the stars
the sea is blue who is the guardian of the sky
you are a ship in the middle of the sea not wrecked by wind or storm
you are a mountain in the middle of the plain you are a lake in the
    middle of a desolate land
you are the *speculum humanae salvationis* you are the ferryman of evil
next to you every light is too modest next to you every sun is dark
every brick every house every crumb every dust
every fiber every blood every mountain every snow
every tree every life every valley every chasm
every hatred every lamb every blaze every rainbow

the occupation, guys, occupation
cats on counters, singer sewing machines
quickly drink beer, ghost, stuff bananas in your mouth, occupation
intestines are spurting, occupation is like the ocean
the bombs of sweet words died, necrophilia
wet icy stones, people hatch like flies one after another
occupation is queues, the screams of soiled widows
occupation is enormous cans of red substances
people squeeze their asses together, sell solidarity
occupation is waving with hands, the crackling of young flesh
of old flesh occupation, the tempo
fantastic occupation, dogs, ants, robbers, blades
occupation is to be torn apart by a wolf in the middle of the street
a bull stomps so that they shoot you with pleading hands like a hostage
crows, black instincts, the bloodshed of apartment owners
oil shortage occupation, ships for the enemy
occupation, lip-smacking, the people speak eternal words
the elevators are stopped occupation, we go for water with buckets
occupation is gold for butter, making flags
marvelous adventures, strengthening the body occupation
occupation is so that you lie in moss for two days and two nights
so that you don't sneeze don't flinch don't kick don't flee
with occupation everything penetrates by day
occupation is scaling the nation after four
risk, silk, the scent of travel
blisters on your hands when you dig soil
an incredibly large shift occupation
white horses, saccharin, cots, haircuts
occupation guys, occupation

jesus christ fries in hell. for a long time his pastured
sheep gave ten kinds of wool. abraham was flying
through the air like a butterfly. when he turned
fourteen and passed his little exams they bought him
motorcycle goggles. at every bath he prayed
he wouldn't be like the dutch. jesus christ said:
do you see all of this? I'm telling you the truth: here
there'd be no stone on a stone that wouldn't be knocked down.
saul still smells of horror and murder.
jesus christ was crucified when he was thirty
three. on the left side was the left thief
on the right side was the right thief.

I see the devil's head, people, I see his entire body
I never thought he could come so close
he yearns for innocence, like us
I have the feeling that he was stuffed into a wall for a long time

I have the feeling that his hands hurt
that he is gentle and pensive, that he licks everything before killing it
he pants and rips when he claws at flesh, he is blessed
he has no friends, he walks the world alone

I have the feeling that he is telling me something
that he is looking at me with regret
he knows I could never sleep with him
we are both humiliated

he reminds me of an english professor after he has retired
of young secret police, it seems his bliss has diminished
souls squeal when he tortures them, he doesn't drink them like I imagined
it seems to me that he has no use for them

I think he would like to have a friend to share goods and pleasure with
he steps into the river and dips his head in it
he doesn't know how to talk to it, he splashes on the surface
I will leave him like that and won't talk to him

RED FLOWERS

red flowers grow in heaven, a shadow is in the garden
light penetrates from everywhere, the sun isn't visible
I don't know how a shadow is in the garden, how dew is on the grass
large white stones are strewn around so that one can sit on them

the hills around are like those on earth
only they're lower and look completely brittle
I think we're completely weightless and barely touch the ground
if I walk, it seems that red flowers recede a little in front of me

it seems that the air is fragrant, that it's terribly cold and searing
I see new beings arriving
as if an invisible hand is setting them on the grass
they're all beautiful and serene and we're all together

some swimming here in the air turn around and break away
they vanish and we don't see them anymore and they moan
it seems that my body is in a bright tunnel
that it rises like dough and then sprinkles the stars apart

here in heaven there is no sex, I feel no hands
but all things and beings are perfectly connected
and they rush apart to unite even more
colors evaporate and all the voices are like a soft lump on the eyes

now I know that I was sometimes a rooster and sometimes a roe
that I had bullets in my body, which crushes them now
how beautifully I breathe
I have the feeling that an iron is ironing me and that nothing is scorching me

I WANT VERSE TAUT

I want verse taut as bamboo
buffalo's anathema, the hard planks of satan
snails' anathema, the slackness of succumbing to wars
worms! I want a hunger carpet at heaven's door

I want fanfare, splendor, kneeling
the priests' service, blindly shaking the flocks
I, a king, want sanctity for the slaughter
from your hands, sir, a pillar for the abyss

I want a scepter, a gift for the black mouth
dry cracking pretzels, the silk of lilliput
I smell mattresses on rusty hooks
brushwood in a lap, I smell wounds in a scream

bread's anathema, the layered grains of dead tribes
ants drowned in marshes, nailed moths
travelers & sailors, juniper, sacred ground
I crush the rubble in souls, drink glory

I am the people's point of view, a cow
a tropical wind, I sleep beneath the surface
I am the aristocratic cannibal, I eat form
I drum on cooks' white caps

I drum on their aprons, I am the green integration
water flows into the lazaretto, ice builds on boots from the moisture
little drums, elementary forces, little snouts
the dog snarls in pictures

the temperature battered, the door, I tossed a gold ring
into boiling oatmeal, autumn is here
fate has the same circle, pedestrians stink
new snow falls on the snowballs

the grasses are soaked in coats of scarlet red
the air swirls, the thicket swirls over the desert
carpets are beaten, color gets up with sunrise
more people will see me, with sunrise I become morning

poetry must be made of music, deftly!
I buried my soul in sand so that it can rest
so that it hides and clings, so that it will be protected
so that satan's teeth will slide when he bites into it

the hymns of giants, covered shoulders
I chopped off my hair, fingers, the black thresholds of pictures
I feed princes, I don't touch the hunting grounds
I die in front of senators, among burning geese

I have powerful blood, plenty of supplies
I smear my mouth with soap so that it screams
if my shadow falls on a shiny metal object I throw myself at it
I don't drop it until I warm it

if the sun comes through the door before the great winters I'm saved
bury me privately, surround the grave with crosses
let me lie down so that time is visible
let my hair and fingers be kept in sealed polyvinyl bags

don't fear images of the world, children, close your eyes
don't fear roads, dead bodies in trees
don't fear screams and valleys, behold
the water doesn't dry up, the skin chars

don't fear grasses, those dead from the plague
don't fear being wrapped in color, angry people
mothers rot and return, angels sleep
blackness awaits you, a white light

don't fear the sand castles around the house
protectors from fire, signs of ridges
you consume blood from sheet metal, salt from a horse's mane
you belong among silence and beasts, among pilgrims of the gates

don't fear towers, fire drills
don't fear miracles, swimming in the wake of a shout
the wings of starving tribes, the screaming of a dream
a guardian angel watches over your night

I ride a horse, black images
I ride relentless words, meek bread
thorns have embedded in my soul, the sand of mules
white birches burn, halls burn

fish burn without air, night without a mouth
sand burns, footsteps burn in sleep
the fresh skin of the world burns, I ride shivering
the strength to die, lord, I watch how he sleeps

I sense the gatekeeper of heaven and earth, I sense the mills
I sense the third day of the flood, the karst burns
the arc of trimmings, networks of dusty roads
I sense you and look at you, enchant and submerge you

where the wall will crumble, we crucify dreams
I crucify my lamb, a golden purse
I crucify the blazing eyes of the buried, the burning vine
I crush hope and footsteps, the gestures of the meek

LEGENDS

Legends, like the most beautiful flowers, grow from black soil.
I open my arms, fall, slide into a wide, soft place;
I don't know what's on the other side, maybe I'll walk to the hill
and reach the pass, where I'll see the valley.

I know that I'm already here, there. I don't know if the landscape
measures and what it measures with; I don't know what floats in it.
I'm tired. Here, suffering recedes in front of people,
I'm like a fish in an aquarium without glass panes.

But this isn't the sea. I laced my boots and prepared
to go out, into the cold and winter. The sun is clear and frail,
it's not its time yet. Everything returns, everything turns,

slowly, silently, as if far, far away you see
a truck rolling down a steep slope.
It floats, bounces, flies in a small arc into the abyss.

On the border between Pennsylvania and Ohio
the sky is higher, the land flatter,
the murdered grain returns like a miracle,
like moss and snow, like silence.

Nature, the word, melts in the mouth
like honey cakes long forged in the dark,
thaws at the roots. Suspicious fields,
silent surfaces, still offer a reflection,

they cover the body with a dead color so they're not
hurt by the quick, indifferent looks of sightseers.
Young, vulnerable tissue is generous only

to friends, devoutly serving the new
balance of the world, the gentle touch of love,
bright kisses light as breath.

Great poets
accurately predict their deaths in one line.
When they tire,
wear down their guardian angel so that it falls asleep,
they pierce the ground with truth.

No hand reaches out and pushes
the omens back into the dark, loved ones sleep
covered by their dreams like a mossy basin.

They don't hear the lightning,
don't rush,
don't flinch at the breakthrough
that strikes the seal and crushes physical presence.

Maruška enchants me and rips me apart before I see her.
In the service of love and fear
she stands cruel as a hunter of dormice,
stops me at the edge with the heavy blow of a club.

I

I, after whom Ljubljana can be called antediluvian
and post-Šalamun, am cheerful, Arabian, so right away I ask
that you forgive my first line.
The homeland, women, bread, and languages of all kinds,
French dreams, state awards, and agaves will appear.
Zoran Kržišnik might even come on the scene,
grandma, grandma's hats,
and how I truly think that Mr. Bucik is a greater painter
than Jakopič because he painted my mother.
What Mrs. Hribar said of my former boss, how
he nationalized the factory:
he was polite, absolutely charming, fucking and communism
shone from his eyes simultaneously, and Izidor Cankar
liked him.
I've no complaints.
And some incredible details from my underground
life that will astound you, wow!
why until my thirtieth year I had become accustomed
to loving everything. I don't have dumplings in my throat.
I have a racket, air to breathe, clumsiness which protects
my soul, and brilliance and Maruška and Ana and friends
whom I sleep with, my body and poetry.
And also terrible pains, which I kick like
a can of milk.
Kardelj, whom I forgive for everything, because he hoped that
Ljubljana would have a million and a half inhabitants because
people will be rushing toward socialism.
Let a person be judged by his dreams.
Toads, honey, the moon, willows, Split, the Baltic Sea, deterioration,
and I'll never forget how we traveled from Krakow to Gdansk.
The chief hires a throng, bribes the head conductor
of the train and then the family sleeps peacefully in first class,
he wakes up with the sun in the north,
with sand, with the Hanseatics, with hawks and eagles
and he bows to the Alps.
Where did they swim, chatting with effendis and Yiddish mamas,
wrapped in scarves and eating cookies with the mayor of Mostar,

where did we sing?
The garden of Mrs. Nardelli and her old Buick absolutely
will be mentioned,
how I was hurt by the conversation with Hewitt,
the John Deere chairman who had breakfast with Tito
and offered him predatory terms for tractors.
He who absolutely appreciates Jagoda Buić
and how in 1880 when the matter started
they were smooth until thirty and then hairy.
And
my dearest friend whose name I cannot
pronounce, Dzoran, does it come from him?
Sure, but not for a fuck, lady, not for a fuck,
and what is this white St. Bernard doing, peeing?
Pascali, that incandescent beast, ships,
Second Avenue, a myth, Third Avenue, light,
where is my dashiki?
There will also be San Domenico Day in Taormina and how
I was smeared when I talked about it with Roy
MacGregor-Hastie, a fascist,
how we threw bombs with Tomaž Brejc in Rome
and fled from the police,
how we still shouted at each other: if they catch us, we'll demand
the embassy, but if all goes well, meet at nine in the evening at
Ivo in Trastevere.
And he said, you are a hopeless Italian, and it was
at five thirty in the morning at Stazione Termini
when he came loaded with books that
I was copying for Jonas for the sacred purposes of the revolution
and I threatened to kill him.
Since then, I fly in planes and look at the earth.
Since then, I have a Social Security Number and am
a renegade.
The greatest Slavic poet. Right.

SAND

I am not the subject,
I am God's cupboard.
Like a cow I must lie on gold
at a precise height.
It's not true that I lie here, on the sand,
because it suits me.
I am the pumpkin on the hot roof of the world,
the Lord drips water on me
so that I don't burn up.
I am not the subject.
I am the pumpkin.
I am not the subject.
I am God's cupboard.
I haven't decided
if I'll look up,
if I'll look down.

GRASS

I want to be so kind that I become a god
and become alone, lost and forgotten.
I compose rhymes because I'm a cactus.
A person is moist to a person,
that's why they kiss on the mouth.
I don't know how to make coffee for myself,
and it's difficult to live with me.
Maruška suffers, Ana doesn't suffer.
As if a tiger were tossing a disc and lazily
playing with it and assessing its height.
But a tiger has no hands and doesn't know this,
it cannot do that, a tiger has teeth and a heart.
Rivers flow through me and fertilize me,
and everything is grass, green grass.
When I'm sad, I get up
and go around the world.
I'm not ready for death,
but I can drink it anytime,
like the soup that Nana gives me.
Death must breathe like a waterfall.
Death must breathe like Mama.
Nothing pungent trudges after me.
Now I'm four years old.
Four and a half,
and I'm the son of the one I love.
If I were older, he'd have to be
over twenty-two years old.
But I want him to forever be as young
and beautiful and terrible as he is today
so that I'll be this old forever.
I'm Russian because he is Russian.
Cindy brought me coffee because I'm so
focused that I shine through the entire house,
onto the garden, into the park, among the squirrels that
Ana will play with when she comes by boat with Maruška.
We'll stay and I'll say:
Ain't no mamba snake in America.

LJUBLJANA

One man goes and falls into a television
and swims over the side and squats by
the television legs like a mosquito. The bill for
the car is twice as much as we expected
and we will pay the mechanic half and
the other half in kisses. Money is kisses
in a freezer, and thawing it into kisses
is a long process. So one kiss
is a hundred bucks. One kiss, a hundred cars,
and we sell them and send them to a foreign currency
account in Ravnikar's bank so that it sprays
outside like air, and every young poet
who eats ice cream in front of the Maxi market,
listen to this stream, drink it,
go home. Write, draw, love
your wife. And people in the Assembly,
this stream is mixed with currant
juice, and already the wisest
laws in the world are accepted and Slovenia
is on top of the world. Maruška, do you see what
kisses create? Worries create wrinkles.
And policemen get new blue uniforms
made from beautiful fabric that breathes, and they say:
hey, comrade, did you see a robber?
But there are no more robbers because they ate
the kisses and they are rocking in a chair
and listening to fairy tales. But the policemen
aren't sad because of this, but happy.
The Party catches cubs from the kisses,
the cubs walk around Ljubljana and lick
people's hands and people caress them
and it's cheerful and they wander down the streets
and there's a parade in Ljubljana and there's a festival.
Maruška, in Ljubljana there's a parade and a festival!
Let's fly home!

HISTORY

Tomaž Šalamun is a monster.
Tomaž Šalamun is a sphere rushing in the air.
No one knows his orbit.
He lies down in twilight, he floats in twilight.
The people and I look at him, astonished,
hope for the best, maybe he's a shooting star.

Maybe he's a divine punishment,
a boundary stone for the world.
Maybe he's such a dot in outer space,
he'll give the planet energy
when oil, steel, and food run out.
Maybe he's only a game of cells, a boil,
and we need to tear off his head like a spider.
But then something would suck up
Tomaž Šalamun, probably the head,
more likely the head than the body.
From the head, new legs would grow.
We'd probably need to squeeze him
between glass, photograph him, and put him
in formaldehyde so that children will look at him
like fetuses, sea nymphs, and human
fish. Doorkeepers would speculate
with tickets and sell them twice.
This is good for people because it gives them a living.
Next year he'll probably be in Hawai'i
or in Ljubljana. In Hawai'i it's very
warm. People go barefoot to the university.
The waves are up to one hundred feet high.
Constantly jolting, jolting the land.
Profiteers rush around town.
The place is fantastic for love
because there is salt in the air and a mild wind.
But in Ljubljana people say: look!

This is Tomaž Šalamun, he went to the store
with his wife Maruška to buy milk
so that he'd have milk to drink.
And this is history.

IMPERIALISM TEARS OFF MY HEAD

In the morning, when I wake up,
I feel that a monster was translated.
That it dissolved, dismantled, and translated itself.
I can no longer call it back,
it lies on the other side, lazy, a pig,
I can no longer call it back.
You no longer eat grass.
The meadow was burned by a welding machine.
You no longer eat my mouth and sound,
you no longer lick my ears, baby.
You no longer breach the sun, you're full,
but you feed on a certain interplanetary
contingent of swamp husks.
Light the fires,
good people of the world,
light the fires.
Before the frost, warm the fields with prayers
that the Slovenian language not be extinguished.
Put a hand on my forehead, Maruška,
be gentle with me, good spirit.
I enchanted you in the open
and loved you with the head of a god,
but you got scared, bride.
I enthroned you, king,
gave you ships and battles,
built you a road to the Hittites, but you were afraid
an elephant would trample you on the way.
Shrunken dried up monkey, deserter, technician.
You were frustrated by the small background.
Lingua franca gives me air.
Lingua franca gives me shelter.
Lingua franca anoints me with oil.
Lingua franca strikes the souls of people like lightning
so that I step in and eat,
so that I step in and eat and enchant and indulge.
Lingua franca tears my head out of this hole
where fat builds up around my body,

where sparks can no longer break through.
Be beautiful, be brave, my language.
Embrace me, hold me,
be on my skin completely,
radiate energy without these shackles.

AIR

Your body is a pipe
through which wheat, oil, and food flow,
a bridge that riders race over.
Your hands are a window,
your words are a window,
your body is a window.
What you touch,
you caress in your mind,
it burns up in terrible flames and smells,
in every gesture,
in every breath you guide me.
And I bow,
and I bow
and I rise
and I rise and go.
You tell me to stop using
swollen, cunning weapons,
hungry, dry weapons of air,
to be careful.
You tell me to be kind and I am kind.
You tell me to be rich and I am rich.
Blue,
my fortresses are mighty
so that I can dart through the souls of kings
and travel from Babylon to Nineveh,
from Nineveh to Babylon.
You designated me:
I am handsome and haughty because I am strong and moist.
Your body is a pipe
through which wheat, oil, and food flow,
a bridge that riders race over.
Your hands are a window,
your words are a window,
your body is a window.

What you touch,
you caress in your mind,
it burns up in terrible flames and smells.

ALONE

One finger is the tundra,
one finger is the Bodhisattva,
one finger is mother Slovenia.
Two fingers still remain, beckoning
and with awful force feeding me
seventeen hands with this arrangement.
Alone,
I'm alone on the roof of the world and drawing
so that stars are created.
I'm spurting through the nose so that the Milky Way is created
and I'm eating
so that shit is created and falling on you
and it is music.
I am God.
I am God and I'm dancing.
This table is a gift, this house is a gift,
this garden is a gift, these squirrels are a gift.
Šekularac's legs are murmuring mantras.
Alone,
alone.
Glug glug glug I'm gulping light
and combing myself. I put all the jewelry down so that I can wash it.
Take a shower and put it back on, alone.
I alone am the center of the world's light, the Lord's lamb.
I alone am all animals: a tiger, an ant, a deer,
a rabbit, a porcupine (hedgehog), a butterfly, an insect,
a piranha, a baby rabbit, a daddy rabbit,
the god of ferrets, the straw hat of a sketched
puppy and his paws.
I alone am all plants: strawberries, birch, hazel,
pumpkin, fern, dandelion, *juves* (*juves* is a plant
with thin roots, resembling the roots
of parsley, but it has a nose and head like
a porcini cap and one birch limb,
sitting all day in a race car like a liana),
maple, oak, corn, alone.
I alone am all the people named in this book

and all the others: Joe, Janet, Agatha, Veronika,
Boris, Ivan, Italo, Pierre, alone.
I alone am the air, smoothly, the lining, two parallel tracks,
pot (to sweat), *pot* (road),
the cause, the forceps, Lope de Vega, the little vein,
the dot on the forehead, the dot in the air, alone.
Alone,
I alone am the air and the golden butter,
linden bark, the king, the sickle and hammer,
the Dalmatian, the saw, Armenia, the key,
alone.

VERGIL

All this twinkling, bubbling, sticky sweet,
soul-flowing decadent sorrel,
love of pouring,
snails set in the mouth, stuck to the heart,
stupor of the marsh.
Stupor of the swamp, swollen from the damp,
from the damp and the heat of a soul longed for,
squeezed by the realization—
they didn't pull me out of Ljubljana
like Caesar pulled you out of the province,
Vergil.
I move quickly,
compactly, duke.
Without sadness and evaporation.
Your misfortune is
that the barbarians were outside,
Rome was empty.
My luck is
that the barbarians are inside the skin of America.
I'm a Hittite.
I don't pay, because I'm high.

TRIESTE

The cafe windows, when I step to the left,
open onto a fishing boat. Trieste is dust.
There's no scent of Italo Svevo and Joyce
anymore, the relatives scattered,
lost money. Their suitcases, silver,
are at Sotheby's, and their ships so
poorly protected that the grandson of the grandsons
of my son Lloyd will be displayed like a dog.
To go gray and soft beside Sekito, a classmate
of Joan's who can no longer compete with her?
To pick daisies and travel for energy.
To listen to the skin, the faces of people
and then decide on what Georgia said: West!
Intentionally? Because she knew that lovers
couldn't leave big cities
and that the air in the countryside will help us?
Because we were afraid that our cells would be
torn apart by an earthquake?
And from this wound, flowers grow. A magnet
that encounters a magnet and gentle
as a lamb swims toward a shooting star.

THE VERMONT ROME AXIS

Technology gushes more than myth and wine.
Summer licks winter and pushes it into the decay of
summer. Winter licks power. A child licks a dog,
and tapestries with twinkling hunters, deer,

brighten the mood of the lord at court. Vermont licks
Romans. Snails, historically undefined, bang
like a torpedo, breaking the balance. The shades in Hades,
innocent as vine tendrils, certainly don't bite.

Then who wreaks havoc, waits for liberation? Who
bites into nature so that they can meet it again?
I think I freeze the river because I'm protecting fish.
I think I eat and kill fish because I'm protecting

the water. A circle that protects a wounded body. Nailed
to the tempo of the stars, they don't hear the sputtering cries:
up! Don't be afraid when I'm awake in this starving,
saturated twilight. Don't be afraid, when

nailed to nature, I hiss tolerance. These are
all stations of a free fuck it, the hunting grounds
of humus, which ripens like the white wings of tiny
snowballs. An arc of calm, not of the maximum.

Perfection is
always circular, not
pointed.

A triangle is
really circular, which is why
it brings such peace.

Sometimes it seems
like history
is stretching out an arm.

This isn't true.
History doesn't have
that power.

I am
infinitely
free.

All my
thinking
is

technical.
Like the thinking
of trees.

Birds
think
only

technically
when flying, the same as
angels.

WRITING

Writing
poetry is
the most

serious
act in
the world.

Just as
in love,
everything

is revealed.
The words tremble
if they are

true.
Just as the body
trembles in

love,
the words tremble
on the paper.

THE WORD

The word is the sole foundation of the world.
I am its servant and master.
And although the soul sends out atoms
that smell, touch, feel, we are truly

in a field where we are equal with the gods.
Language touches nothing that
would be new. There is no final judgment,
no higher one. The Assumption is

in the concentric, where all we see
and don't see is more than a grain
of sand. Things stared at seem closer,
but that is not the criterion. I repeat: things

are not the criterion. The criterion is
in us like the ultimate dissolution.
Death is only a defect in naming
those the light was concealed from.

THE NORTH

The North, which faces north, is stern and blunt
like a flash. Seemingly harsh, silent and swift,
aggressive and white, seemingly full of magnesium,
a waterfall in a vacuum, I say. It weaves and weaves, I give.

In the middle of the process my thoughts wander to cigarettes,
which I forgot break the membrane and hurt
concentration. They push off their backs on their own, push
off my shoulders on their own, jump and crash on their own

like an unfinished body, which at first arouses
more interest than a proper one because of the noise,
because of the white froth crashing, and the North,
which faces north, is already here, stern and blunt. It sticks

to the white froth, which it recognizes because *Up!* can be
imprinted in it. Peace is every discourse, like the chunk of steel
that trains speed along. Which is the North, which
faces north, stern and blunt like a flash.

EPISTLE TO THE ANGRY

My brain is butterflies, a tender precious mass,
diaphanous silk. Swinging your clubs can really
hurt them, or at least ruin the day. Can you imagine
a butterfly that must struggle with the strategy of armored

units holding back such an enraged monster as Mr.
Trampuš, whom I love in principle? Every missed beat
is a sin, every missed rest on a flower, a classic
example of social pathology. My brain is the universe,

wider than blueness. It looks kindly at the sharks
struggling with their sea salad since God gave
all small animals under the sun the right to food.
But between sea salad and a phoenix there are miles,

long miles. A shark isn't even a dolphin, able
to dart through the air in a graceful arc and snap up
some common flying fish, so it will die hungry if
it tragically selects from such an impossible menu.

TURBINES

A planet that repents is a planet that cracks.
The mouth, the turbines are abandoned. Honey drips
and when I discovered that they were iron
rings for horses, I took the purple casket

and glued the pronoun together again. Maybe it'll be
useful to us like the fern is useful.
For fleas, for iron, for Jesus Christ.
Father and son, dismembered, father and son, wrapped

in the same sack. Jesus Christ succeeded.
Peter squashed his dick and remained
the manager; planes, which are present

in all the gaps and cracks, a descriptive
geometry, devoured by exhaustion.
The land is nervous, but the mind is a spine.

CAR LE VICE

Car le Vice, rongeant ma native noblesse,
is guilty of this snarling, of flapping wings.
All day I brag and whoop and dance,
when the sun sets, I'm stunned: a white square of white blueness,

hit with a harpoon like a whale. A little pin,
little as a diamond, makes a histological preparation
from my soul. Hey! how do you even survive,
my dearest, how do you recover?

Such incredibly pathetic questions
Tomaž Šalamun asks his soul to get to
the bottom of things. But there are no things. No bottom.

Just this instructive tale about the creative process
with which sooner or later every immortal destroys
its observers. So that it may float in peace, *il Terribile*.

SPLENDID FASCIST DREAMS

The day will come when I bite into your
eye, Ra. The golden layers gather
around me like a mandorla. I am intensely
fond of this beauty. It breathes. Shrinks

like a stomach, like asphalt. It's good
that nature censors me, imagination
sometimes steals all terrain between 5 and 15
meters high and eavesdrops on lightning.

Some kind of spaghetti is gushing, torn off
in Pascal's interspaces. Signs
that galaxies cease. Yesterday
I smoked too much. People, sentimental

and noisy (30% of Slavs at the party),
rushed for the better cognacs and
representatives of races that have a nimbus
around their heads. In Ethiopia they teach children

affection for women. Today there's oil
on those beaches where Mussolini
sprayed his body like some hamster.
Why all of this? D'Annunzio lost

an eye. Then we talked about
rugs that roll under your feet
and that you must surrender to, or pant
all your life over technology.

SPLEEN

Spleen in a Romanian space is surely the most
rancid butter that a sleeve has ever
caught. Spoiled meat in a Slavic
sandwich, spoiled bread on spoiled

meat—no wonder that this one doesn't go
back among that suffocating folklore.
In a flash you have to create a platform
for how to react to divided sadness

and quench the cynicism of small nations. Finns
have saunas, Hungarians horses. Their silence
is okay. But that's why I'm still frozen stiff
that we operate on all these tumors with bombs.

NIGHTMARE

Nightmare! You are black like the sky.
Black like a clear cool night.
Black like a clear cool gesture,
a meter-ship.

Nightmare! There are beasts on your trunk.
Heavy sacks, axles of sand.
A bloody fire supported by a board,
like we support the house with a board
when we carry it.

Nightmare! You shriek like eyes.
You shriek like Egypt turned on its back.
Like beads of compressed steam. Boards.
Like the oily lips of a jackal
in the orbit of a pearl.

SWANS

When I was little, I thought
arias were some kind of living creatures
with wings. I thought the dark
smoke of carbide billowed from
the score and hands dried out
if they darted too much around the piano.
Students wear bowties
and drink a lot. Doctors make
people out of clay and put them
on shelves. They lick their fingers, smear
children with Pasteur's green
foam. Then life comes
like moles under grass. You cannot
poop and write an opera. They seized
all of grandfather's guns because
he shot his secretary. Kardelj gave
Tic Tac a passport. Now there's
a war in the forests and on the soil.
The Red Star will prevail. Mr. Filip
snores in the bunker because he's a bachelor.
People shouldn't be splashed with a splash.
If you go into internment, a man
whistles and they throw you on a truck.
Father considers children in glass boxes
better guests. Their hands are
bound with raffia. Tito and Pasteur
have huge shoulders. Swans eat
bread and splash.

PAINTED DESERT

When we arrived at the Painted Desert
in Arizona, I remembered Heidegger.
I said to Maruška: I want to go naked
in this sun through the desert,
I remembered that fearful film
by Antonioni, but I was still tempted
to be naked in the sand. Maruška
said: moron! Do you think that I'm going
to watch you vanish at the horizon
and then pursue you with the car
across this sand.
No, I said, we'll both go.
What will happen with Ana, Maruška said.
We'll leave her in the car and give her
cookie. Cookie was at that time
still a drink for Ana. But the desert
will tempt us and we'll never
return, Maruška said.
It's really dangerous, I said, but
your maternal instinct will prevail
and soon you'll come rushing back to Ana.
We had rented a 1972 Chevrolet Impala
with such strong air conditioning that we could
keep the temperature at 60° Fahrenheit.
Chase me through the sand with the Impala.
Too dangerous, Maruška said, but
I opened the door and started
to tear off my clothes because
I remembered Heidegger and Ed Dorn,
who has been living on cocaine now for three years.
All his relationships were relationships
with junkies. Ack! How hot and dizzy
the sand was! The desert is
a fantastic orgasm, more intense than
a woman. Ana grinned madly and
the sky was nearly black, black air.
The Painted Desert is pink, which is why

it has that name, but if you stand on the sand,
the sand isn't pink, it's just diabolical.
If you lie down on the sand, the sand is
diabolical.
God knows if I know I act through codes.
It flashed through me and I remembered
that once, when I still lived with Braco
in those rooms in Gradišče,
I pretended I was Gregor Samsa with such
monstrous peace and sobriety
so much of the time that Braco turned
paler and paler, I asked for
a salad and we went together down the street
because Braco thought it would
sober me up, but I kept
stopping passersby and saying
I was Gregor Samsa and I wanted
a salad, so Braco became
quite ashenly pastel and
convinced that I had gone crazy,
and really, if he hadn't hit me in the head
with his fist in front of the nuns' church
so that I became dizzy and
furious, God knows if I would have come down
at all, and then Braco started vomiting
and I knew he really loved me.
I didn't know that all this could go
so far. I jumped back into the car.
Maruška was just like bronze,
and Ana, who was starting to perceive
in her little head that this wasn't
funny, was wailing. Maruška was
entirely composed, only her body
trembled, and she calmly
drove the car like some hearse
thirty miles south on Route
66 and stopped at a gas
station. With her hands attached to
the steering wheel, she said get dressed, and I

got dressed and I knew:
she is certainly not a witch, she's fond
of you, you fool, one day this
exhibitionism will tear you apart.
Then we spent five days
in the Grand Canyon, calm and gentle,
and I constantly photographed
Maruška, so the most beautiful
photographs are from America, when Maruška
is standing on the edge of the Grand Canyon
in that beige crocheted dress
we bought on Stari Trg, and I
bought her a Hopi bracelet and a Hopi
ring, Ana plenty of ice cream.

TO THE GENTLE EYES OF BAMBI,
TO THE HOLY FATHER

Around a real Pope there is never
a desert, just lively cardinals
who feast on chickens. The oasis
is certainly not the Horn. People live

in a tree or in a box, but
a Pope changes his location with a lift.
Cola di Rienzo was unhinged.
Savonarola was bold but

childish. No one is as enormous as
a Pope, who constantly pushes
the lift button. A Pope presents himself
to the pious as sincerely good. Intelligent

people spit him out like pear seeds;
they shake their democratic heads.
But a Pope is really just like Boeing.
His white cap is hydraulic.

SONNET OF POWER

Let lips and flesh remember the arrival
of a bright and fresh empire. Let it
be squeezed into the eyes and memory: playing with wine
and the flight of bees is for Pilate, not for pathetic
craftsmen. Let this massaging of people's hearts
and the dripping of stalactites on their wide,
unschooled intestines receive its stamp on the green.
grass: obliteration. I thus had them
compose this diet of delightful and thrilling
reading. Let them also become little
schoolkids so that this impatient stomping on the ground
settles down and submits to the natural state of things.
The events really inspired me. So let
the board with my office hours be hung up publicly.

THE LIFE OF A POET

Love tore apart all my theories.
The stars devoured me.
I'm anonymous, what I always wished for so badly.
I am light, a tiny strand of light.
It's truly fantastic how the stars eat me.
Again and again, what endless food I am.
And then: pink!
I touch some hair,
pink! I write a poem, expand eternity.
Like here now: the Yaddo castle is an outpost for the renewal of the world.
I look at a tree: I see, I sense, I know
I love Maruška, Maruška loves me.
A ladybug flies to my shoulder.
That's Ana.
Now she is painting or walking in puddles
with her mommy and saying:
"I won't have a birthday until Tomaž returns."
And a beautiful, multicolored bird crashes into my window,
the souls of friends, connected in a gentle net around the planet.
None of them is jealous of each other
because we're all lovers.
Then I take ten letters to the post office, only love letters.
For overseas, for here.
Poets are made by physical contact and reading.
Junk! Junk! we splash into the sun.
All this goes too quickly for philosophers.
They think we are a bit crazy and simple-minded
because we use language like children.
Hey, you, blockheads, tedious pedestrians!
Wouldn't the world be more exquisite
if you were more physical toward your masters?
Boom! boom! the kisses of the people fall on my head.
What a bang.
I hope that I'll hang on,
that I'll be able to return all this love forever.

The history of heaven is massive,
you don't have to drink anyone's blood.
Blood is censored sperm,
a symbol that maintains the temperature
with a dislocated image.
You alone must decide
if you'll step here or not.
I'm just a speck.
I have no scent, no flavor,
no color, no shoulders.
I'm not such that crucifixion
could make me Jesus Christ.
I didn't steal the flowers
when I planted them in the soil.
I'm on absolutely no one's list.
I'm not an engine that needs
to burn gasoline
or run between the moon and the sun
like a brahmin.
I'm a pure spirit,
without consequences.
The history of heaven is undone by me.
Forever at the disposal of people, cats,
flies, spiders, roses, and lilies.

FEAST

On the path of all spheres,
on steep cliffs overgrown with segments of color,
marked with the chalk that children
broke, we watch the pieces
rising,
compact as if under the pressure of water,
their slow takeoff: *markings*,
white curtains raised.
There are no problems with breathing,
right here, in this circle,
there are no problems with breathing
and also ahead, in front, it seems
as if equilibrium is built in, unbreakable;
cavities constantly expand,
expand and narrow,
as the activity of an unknown (imaginable)
respiratory system enlarges under a microscope.
Nostalgia, night, melancholy, laughter
falling like snow are invalid,
all *parallel*, *all there*, which can be
reached from *here*, the entire "path" in between.
We watch the reactions to this situation,
slowly, gradually, the outer leaves of an artichoke
slowly float away.
We can imprint any memories of the concepts.
There was a line.
It was there exactly because we couldn't
use it.
Whatever the concept, they're all arranged
concentrically, near, far.
The spot, which was an elevator, a beam,
is protected in advance by inviolability.
Initiation is unbelievably slow work,
most similar to the rotation of summer, winter, and the stars.
Is this how we ate?
Did we constantly prepare food?

Now it's enough that a small crack in the process remains
and everything regenerates unbelievably fast.
Whoever keeps a diary of growth and sacrifice,
look!
Maybe many can read it
because light *falls* around,
but of course nothing falls here, it goes outward.
The center, the source of energy that we observe in this
process, is *empty*. The universe "vanishes" the locus, eats it.
Energy, not consciousness, leaps, (is) in the negative.
So it's *all* in something, which, because
of the concept, can be roughly called a grain of sand
and the entire space is only a vestige,
like sawdust from sawing wood.
In one cubic micromillimeter
there are infinite galaxies, and *each* with this huge
space, with nights, moons, suns, with constellations
that baffle us and press our membrane.
Intergalactic, and, of course, these
"injected" communications are also just pressure.
Beside this window, in this window
there are still countless other civilizations,
countless other cosmological systems.
So it's not about suffering,
but about layers.
I'm showing this here.

ACQUEDOTTO

I should have been born in 1884 in Trieste,
at the Acquedotto, but couldn't manage it.
I remember a three-story pink house,
a furnished parlor on the first floor,
and my great-grandfather, my father,
how tense and alert he was every morning
reading the stock market news, blowing cigar smoke
into the air and quickly calculating.
When I had been inside my great-grandmother
for four months, there was a meeting, which delayed
my arrival for two generations,
the decision written down on a dazzling sheet
of paper and placed in an envelope, sealed
and sent to the Viennese archives.
I remember that I decided to travel
back toward the light, turned there on
my stomach and saw how a tall, elderly
man muttered, eyed a shelf, took someone
from a neighboring shelf, and shoved
his head toward a chute of air.
I think I was seven years old,
the replacement, my grandpa,
may have been older, nine or ten.
I was calm, but at the same time these events shook me.
I remember that I was wasting away for a while,
probably because of the too-strong light,
then my lungs, like some bags
held out beautifully, arrived the day
I attained the necessary muscle tone and I fell asleep.
I knew that was my body down below
and I saw it in my sleep several times.
It was a man of slow movements, with a mustache,
all his life a dreamer, though a banker.

I challenge
leaders to be gentle.
Why must I

live in a world
that detests
spirituality?

Why can I
write barely
20% of my poems

at home
and must forever
fly

from the land
that I'd like
to love

the most
so that I don't suffocate?
Why do I feel

this irrational
dislike,
this fear

of freedom
and human dignity?
This poem is a personal

petition
and a suit.
It stems from the shock

and horror
that I experience
over and over

when being licked
by domestic traumas.
That's how many

of us feel.
This is a petition
and suit

for all of us
seasonal
workers.

Whoever reads me
as ironic
will be guilty

before God.
I don't care about
your decadent

defense systems,
all this embossed
criminal shit

you proclaim
to be humor and
the cornerstone

of your
historical
experience.

HYMN OF WORLDWIDE RESPONSIBILITY

I proclaim the brotherhood of natural, strong, sacred people.
A bond of incandescence, a bond of blazing lightning, bright labor,
the mind and soul of the planet, we are, like you,
a conspiracy of delight, smaller than a drop of blood.
We (I and you and rain and dust),
we (deer and door and cries and slow snails),
we who've shed all our dead surfaces
heal the wounds of human hearts.
We are not hostile to the fire of all ages, all movements.
We proclaim the ripeness of the world, its everlasting growth and
      permanence,
its quiet footsteps in the snow and roaring waterfalls,
we proclaim the sacred language as forever spoken by the people:
I'm afraid, I'm happy, I love you, let me eat.
May everything erupt on a clear day, just as it is,
into sacredness and the beauty of the gift: life.
You decadent tunnels,
minor masters of closed sacks,
weary slaves of a despondent refinement that speculates
on goals,
we invite you to a dance.
Ever since the sun has shone in the sky, a child's tear was clear.
You, whom sparks crumpled into a million
cubic miles of fear,
don't be afraid,
our divine rain will wash you off.
We bring love and freedom without hatred.
And you, vampiric language,
who betrayed the body out of a passion to populate
unknown countries:
wrong!
Dance with us, be a brother,
all the colors are gathered in our hearts.

I LOVE YOU

The history
of heaven's growth
is the movement

of every eyelash
on every
born and unborn

human face.
Neither kittens nor
trees

nor herds
of wild animals
are excluded

or forgotten.
The history
of heaven's growth

is the image
of all pastures,
the image

of all the shadows on the green
pastures
in the glow and the dark.

Every pain
of every trembling
of the earth is

every cry
of all the children set down
at birth.

Don't worry
don't worry, Maruška,
rest in grace.

The history
of heaven's growth
is

every drop
of the rainbow
that falls on your forehead,

that quenches,
spreads yearning
and love.

SONNET OF MOTION

Stories that have a first scene, a second
scene, a first border, a second border, surrender like
a lump of meat. The brain slips and smacks its lips.
Radical light is always muscular,
it eliminates situations where you can look back.
And from its head leaps another material,
untouchable thoughts. And the swift chamois that
crouches mid-leap, ledges that
consume consciousness and stay
far behind, restraining their scent and
terror—musk. Is the chamois gone, where's
the chamois? He stood a meter, like a notion
of whiteness. Don't search here because
I've spoken. There's consistently nothing here.

I stepped into a town with
three bell towers.
The bell on the first was white,
the bell on the second was black,
the bell on the third was green.
In my gloves I carried
cows and crickets, so my nail
was swollen.
I bit it off
with my teeth, a traitor, an Atlas
who transformed my
pain into frivolity.
After that I had a well
in my finger. I poured it out on
the people's red cheeks.
They spat and croaked like
poor frogs,
in a rush all their lives,
never at the top of the bell tower,
never above the ringing of the bells.

Is explicitness a wound?
Is power then
the wound of a wound? Cold indifference,
as long as the trench lasts, the power plant
under construction, water
accumulating behind concrete,
the production of energy is a reduction
in nature.
What resists the theft of land?
Does the dam really resist?
Do birds return to
the convex eye? Does an earthquake knock down
a wall? You are trust, freedom,
an emperor. The victims are the submerged
villages, their residents and
I—the locals—
under
the most fatal attack
of rage—rage alone—
a container that holds up as long as it isn't
torn apart by the pressure.
I'm the last measurement.
The final reflection of the instrument
itself in the chain of total
annihilations.

I'm a machine loved by
fatal rage. You don't recognize me
when I comb and stroke my hair,
when I flip dry hay
and sing like a robust happy
farmhand. I'm a machine, blind and deaf.
In my huge ears I have
tufts of fresh flowers,
butter on my velvety
red lips. My militant
beard has a hole. Whoever
sees it as a wrinkle—and how
shall I otherwise stand in the field of belief—
hangs like a shank in my
heavy smoke, like
a bat in my
violet sunrise.

I saw how the planet fell.
Hands became bumblebees.
Apples sharpened my teeth
in the first age of gold.
Bumblebees became foil.
The foil is recorded as
A, as B, as C.
Like an atom, which is really
a hieroglyph.

My race is always pelting
a little owl with stones.
It doesn't eat,
doesn't sleep,
stays awake all night.
My race guzzles
entire carts of sand.
It hires a winemaker
and dismisses him,
sees a thorn in his heel
and kills him.

Historical brutality,
you're a poppy.
With a black scepter, silk
wings.
I see everything: the field
of dew and castles'
wedding guests.
Enchant me then, rabble,
I'm opening the leaves.
Drink me like wine,
say moooo.

I WRITE EVERYTHING DOWN

I write everything down, all the deaths.
I see that you recognized me.
I'm gilded under people's eyelids,
my hands float.
My fear killed
you, the avalanche
collapsed. I'm
a sacred cow licked naked
by calves. I no longer have countless udders.
Now I'm holding onto
a shroud, my elbow touches the shroud
through my shirt, sphinx. Suffering is
tender and clear. Pleasure is
a roaring stove that clarifies the morning.
A certain woman goes over the pavement, most likely
wearing sandals.
I'm always clumsier in my joy, in my
generosity. I see you with some strange piece
of meat beneath your shirt,
you are resting and serene like
a mask. Did you roll up those maps
of the sky, did you take them away?
I pierce the air with a finger because I'm watching if
it thickens. Sometimes I think it will thunder. Like some
stump or bronze, and now I will go into someone else's
circle. I continuously check if I still have
the canteen by my side—
you were a soldier too—
so that I'll be able to drink.
I was your Angel of Debauchery.

A truck
hurtles through the saturated
air. The asphalt is

greasy but
I cannot see it. I know
the anguish of Slovenia.

It spins and
softens what's in the middle
of the window frame:

unformed
dark karstic stones
placed on

glowing
neutral red
bricks. A leaf

has
greater compactness than
the birth

of an angel, even
if it falls carefully into the mouth
of a green aphid.

The day
deepens.
The earth

rises
with a silent blast
like a net.

The body is
a signal, a window
that agrees

with the door.
The corridor
of dazzling light

is long.
What else are we missing
from the field?

HUNGER

I know
hunger,
it stands at

the threshold.
Hunger is
a vagabond

and a muzzle,
an ugly turtle.
I didn't push

you away.
Hunger, you're
a deadbeat.

I caressed
you,
classified you.

DOG

Dog! What are you doing with your hair?
You wallow in the mud like some pig.
You stand up and spatter me
and blink and yawn.

Dog! Who was your mother,
don't you have brothers and sisters? Did they
all leave you and fall asleep behind some
corner? You're hungry. Lazy and feral.

Dog! I've never seen you before.
You run down the road and stop, you run
down the sidewalk and down the road again.

Stars will fall on your head,
you're weird. Leave that case of
canned food alone. Dog! You are so weird!

KLUTZES

A woman is howling like a dragon because I'm a poet. No
wonder. Poetry is a sacred machine, the lackey
of a faceless deity that kills on an assembly
line. How many times I'd already be
dead if I didn't have
languor, calmness of spirit, and
arrogance in me so that
I blot out the wings with my
instruments. Fly, fly forward, sacred
object, that's not me, I'm reading
Delo and drinking coffee with workers in blue
jumpsuits. They also could kill
themselves when they climb up poles and install
electricity. Sometimes they actually do. Poets often kill
themselves. I was killed by too-strong words
scrawled on a piece of paper, *my*
vocabulary did this to me. But
no one will tell me that these aren't
klutzes. Klutzes are in all
professions. Any pedestrian can kill
himself if he doesn't know what
a crosswalk is.

ETHER

I.

My hands are tied with a rope, at the ends
there's wood. The sky is violet and brown.
When I see this, it doesn't touch me.
I feel the fingers on both hands.
I hear a car passing by.
Wool sips me. I'm a lamb.
A lot of salt is in the air, the mistral is blowing.
Semicircular arches are being made from the light,
like a wide rainbow, from me. I no longer have
any weight and maybe this will lift me up.
Then I won't write anymore. I grease,
weigh down my body so I can write.
I see only the first three circles. I cannot
look further up because of
the melting. It disperses, no longer visible.
The word is a weapon that protects me from
the path. Now I'm not a lamb, I have
a hand, I caress the grass. In my ears I have
the feeling that I've been in the sea
a long time. I'm thinking. I see a house.
Accounts of this are a defense against
annihilation.

II.

Geniuses and angels slide out of people's
noses. At first they're like
embryos, then like pupae opening
their fibers. I lean over for a cigarette.
I clench my teeth and clutch my knees
with my palms. The lord of desire is
blue, not monolithic. In the east they
highly valued silk because it resembles
this air. I have no defense.

I'm placed in safe hands. I want
to be hungry so that this ends.
On the horizon, a black dog swims
as if there were water, but there's no water.
It chews my hand, but it doesn't hurt.
The black dog is quite mellow. I'm artificially
creating fear. Fear is a work of art.
I'm vicious. I pour a pail of water
over my head. All this has no
taste, the colors have their
locus, their origins. They
populate my body like ether.

III.

Sometimes cobwebs are on words.
Sometimes filaments, sometimes salt.
Now there's bark and knots and a screeching
knife. I always go clothed here,
not naked. I imagine that I
know how much it can puff in my head.
I really have no idea. Sometimes I throw
the knife into the veil so that I can get it
back. Under the skin is a second skin,
under the second skin is a third skin.
I see the end of the street. I can count
everything: two candelabra. I see
a grid made from the lattice of Sol LeWitt.

IV.

The curves drive me to sleep,
a child dies.
On the altar there's eggnog,
I'll stay, I'll stop.
God, grant me rest,
in the cave,
in the rain.

HISTORY IS A WOMAN, LET'S BE GAY (II)

Tracts from political economics

God, you're stealing language and paper from me.
The work has become your body.
I kill you, I kill myself, I love you,
I love myself. Give me a gangplank, lightning.
I'm blind. I'm mute.
I lie on the sand, full of jewelry.
You are under the fingers, under the fingers.
Some bunny will hop by, or some farmer
will roll a tire. I'll eat
with a spoon, I'll always eat with
a spoon. In heaven there are shock rooms,
a flame that people waft on
the roe. I'm your parallel man,
I'm your parallel man.
I anoint you so that nothing costs you,
so that you'll be mine. Legendary is the space between your
thumb and middle finger, a silent assault when the thing
falls. Why hasn't it until now? Why are you still holding
me? I don't believe I'm
mortal when I'm looking at you, when I'm caressing you, when I'm
eating you.

FOLK SONG

Every true poet is a monster.
He destroys the voice and the people.
His singing builds the technology that destroys
the earth so that the worms don't eat us.
A drunkard sells his coat.
A scoundrel sells his mother.
Only a poet sells his soul
to separate it from the body that he loves.

MONSTRUM (LAT.) FROM THE VERB *MONSTRARE*

I contribute to the story because no
doubt there will be plenty of theses on who I am.
My life is clear and named
just like my books are named.
I'm also alone, like you, voyeur. And
I also wince if someone
sees me. I'm looking you in the eyes. We both know
the question. Who kills? Who remains? Who
looks? This one, who furiously tears off
his clothes to be innocent, isn't
this a pretense? Your heart beats because my
blood beats. Wrong. My heart beats because your
blood beats. You have the same right as I do,
who is your guardian angel, your monster.

TRIUMPHAL ARCH

Yesterday afternoon Giorgio came to me
again. I took him to lunch.
He showed me the poems he wrote
that morning. Then he phoned Alfonso
at San Luis Potosi, 113A. Alfonso
said he'd wait for us on Calle Jalapa,
but we missed him. We went to
his old colonial house and waited
in front of it. He arrived in a Volkswagen,
his head shaved. I immediately knew he was a wizard.
He seemed to be very interested in me.
He led us around the rooms, we talked
about Lévy, Sir Randolph. He told
me about his zen master and showed me
the book he was finishing: Worldwide Nutrition
Plan. Then we smoked something
he said was ordinary grass from Palenque.
I grabbed his things, swords,
orbs, crosses made of rope, played with
mercury in vials. He said
he would put on a little show for us.
He danced, acted, and panted, grinning
constantly in between. You'll be amazed at
the terrible power that kills, he said.
You won't be able to resist delight.
Now I'll get on with writing the book,
he said, and drive you downtown.
We got out at the Niza-Hamburg
intersection. We started to walk. I was amazed
that I was taking such big steps, that I
breathed so deeply, that I moved so
harmoniously. Where are we going? I asked
Giorgio. Let's go, he said. Are you afraid?
I asked him. He said he was sure
I wouldn't kill him. I didn't know anymore.
I had the feeling that a force would
lead us through the temple so that I would eat

his heart. We went somewhere
to sit down and drink something because
our mouths were very dry. We walked along
the carpet. We arrived at Avenida Juarez,
Giorgio pointed out the huge triumphal arch
at the Plaza de la Republica. There's my
hotel, he said. We walked a kilometer
on the red carpet, a huge flag fluttered
on the triumphal arch. It was the 20th
of November, a Mexican holiday. Where are we going?
I asked him. To the beginning, he said.
Everyone will be there, the president of the republic and
the king of Spain, too. I only felt how
my strength increased, how I would first
make love to him and then eat his heart. You know,
he said to me, Alfonso told me that a snake
once passed in front of him. He backed away,
the snake moved toward him. When he
gave it all his strength, it didn't kill him. Does it seem
to you like I'm that snake now, I asked
him. No, he said, you aren't the snake.
You walk parallel with me. He pointed
his finger to the right, down the carpet, which
led to the eternal flame under the triumphal arch,
and I became sad. Then we walked for another
hour or two, always with
the temple on the left or the right, I remember
the sound of a flag fluttering. Then he
pointed at a window, this is my window.
You decide, he said. Hotel Pennsylvania
was all tiled, covered in blue
enameled tiles. An old woman was sleeping
at reception. In the room when we were
smoking, he said, you decide, it's
up to you whether you kill me or not.
I stopped unbuckling my belt. I stopped
taking off my boots. I lay down and
fell asleep. When I woke up, Giorgio
was crying. He was sitting on a raffia chair

pressed against the wall. You aren't the only one
who'd like to love, he said. I sensed that it was
finished. I'd drunk his heart. I'm going
now, I said. Giorgio's face was
beaming and handsome. You see, he said,
reassured. The light is for everyone. This
morning when I went to breakfast and
bought the *Unomásuno* newspaper, I read
that in the jungle of Guyana
383 Americans had committed ritual
suicide under the direction of Jim Jones.

16.III.1979

In the tomb of the ancestors Alejandro Gallegos
Duval smells of warm damp salt. I ride
horses. I'm learning. When will I lose
enough so that I'll sober up?
I see fear in people's eyes. Does
nature sustain me because it also burns from
the casualties? Three days ago, when I
left the house to buy a ticket
for Slovenia, the landlady stopped me
and gave me a telegram.
HAVE WARNED YOU. STAKES WERE HIGH.
GAME WAS ONE. HAVE LOST EVERYTHING.
                    WHAT I AM
GETTING IS TO SUPERFICIAL. STAY AND
ENJOY YOUR BOYS AND CHEAP THRILLS.
METKA—
BAD GIRL: OBVIOUSLY NOT TIME FOR
MARRIAGE NOW, I answered with a dry
throat. We know this. This, which takes your
breath away, is called a crisis. The earth
collapses, sorrow blows, and there are plenty
of new fields. Alejandro's eyes are always
deeper. His paintings are called
ŠALAMUN I ŠALAMUN II ŠALAMUN III

How are yours? I only still love and
sleep. I don't know who balances
the hours of my protagonists. I also wrote:
more information that might interest you.
At the time you sent your telegrams, there
was a 7.0 magnitude earthquake here. Every other
city would topple to the ground, but not
Ciudad, because it's built on water. The color
of the sun that I faithfully gathered on my
skin for the wedding, you see? No investment.

DEAR METKA!

Every morning I've had fresh flowers on my tablecloth.
Now they're replaced in large vases
every other day. During breakfast I sit at
the Quiet Table, so I just raise my hands and
wave my fingers when I'm greeted
because I'm afraid metaphysics would escape me
if I said good morning. No one here
suffers because of you or Alejandro.
I'm always telling Patricia, Allan
and Kathy that I am afraid you won't get very
much out of me, I am just married—
April 11—and on the way to be with my
Mexican lover. Everyone here is fond of you.
I dance with Kathy, walk among fireflies
with Allan—we go through the woods as on
a carpet—and I admire Patricia madly
because of the paintings. When I make love with her,
I become the tree that she draws. Don't be
sad if I repeat to you that
I won't be able to live with you, as
people call it, "faithfully." I tried
and changed my plans. I'll be in
Mexico from the twenty-second to the twenty-ninth,
not from the twenty-ninth to the sixth.
So the week before I fly to
Ljubljana I'll rest here again and
it won't be like when I flew to
the wedding and the space of time between
the moment I knocked on
Dalmatinova and the moment
I kindly pushed Alejandro out of bed at
Salina Cruz was only fourteen hours.
I'm afraid it would scare you
to death again.

GOD

I demand
unconditional
love
and
total
freedom.
That's why
I am
terrible.

With my tongue,
like a loyal devoted
dog, I lick your
golden head,
reader.
Terrible is my
love.

GAUZE

When I'm 37 years old, I won't be
bald. I won't
wear white robes with red
intestines in the pocket.
When I'm 37 years old,
my mother won't die. I won't
knock on the doors of my sons' rooms with
foolish questions on a foolishly happy
face.
When I'm 37 years old, I won't
exercise at half past five
in the morning and whistle through my nose like
a maniac. I won't
towel off in village
inns and offend pious
people after they barely survived
the war. I won't
wear knickers. I won't
bring up Haloze and everything they took
from us and say
it's right.
When I'm 37 years old, I won't
be on duty, but
free. I'll let myself grow a long beard and long
nails, my white ships will sail all the world's
seas. And if a woman
gives birth to my children, I'll throw them through
the windowpane from the left corner
of the dining room and wonder
what will fall on the pavement first,
the glass or the gauze.

CIRCLES

My
rings are made from
yellow

gold,
from white gold and
silver.

I have wives under
glaciers and among
palm trees.

Who pays
me for such
a life!

My
Slovene nation? My
Slovene

nation
already knows what it's doing. And even
an enemy

who'd like
to meddle with my Slovene
nation

is informed.
Everyone knows: what I
write

really happens.
His head would immediately
fall off.

EPITAPH

There's only God. The spirits are an apparition.
The blind shadows of machines that obscure the Kiss.
My Death is my Death. I don't share it
with the blunt stillness of others annihilated under the sod.

Whoever kneels on my grave:
the earth will shake. I will extract sweet juice from
your neck and genitals. Give me your mouth.
Be careful so that a thorn doesn't pierce your

eardrum. When you wallow like a worm,
alive in front of the dead. Let this oxygen bomb
wash you gently, gently. Let it explode you only

as much as the heart can bear. Rise and
remember: I love everyone who knows me.
Always. Now rise. You surrendered and awoke.

PRAYER

Friend!
Have you ever experienced
the infinite delight of stars
commingling,
the bursting of a flower as it
opens at the red
horizon?
Don't underestimate the most
terrifying aesthetic
pleasures.
Every day, every
minute I fight
for you.
Thank you for
the name.
It's my last
ally in the battle for your
life.
Pray for me.
Pray that the enemy doesn't dazzle
my mind and drag me
innocent into
the machine.
Pray that I control time in
sleep and keep you alive with
silence.

THE LIGHT NOT FED FROM LIGHT

Smell of blossoming buckwheat,
why are you tempting Transylvanian vampires?
Shears are an instrument that hurts.
No one has the right to break a stone,

to move a door from east to north.
And yet: archaeologists discover wrought
iron. How to topple responsibility?
It's growing into a pandemic. A creature,

staring into fire for the first time, sizzled,
the burning was terrible, even in the rain,
and coveted it for himself: destiny is in desire.

A tree burned joyfully. Whoever *preserves*
life enlists. Only someone who cuts
a mirror with a diamond can sleep peacefully.

ORANGE JUICE

I'm exhausted. After a long night
the grass is gray from dew. The spruces are
ballerinas. I forgot my lunch box
in the bedroom. If the wind

stopped, a cloud would fall into the pond.
My boot is dark brown from
water on the ground, which comes from the sky.
I'm absent-minded and infected by the glow.

I'd surely be more loyal than
a monk in the Tang dynasty. Loves
that drift so quickly. Death is

a strange beverage. Like the papers
pinned at the tailor's, encircled by chalk.
Like the white clouds around the tops of the spruces.

MEMORY

In the cry of
heaven I hear
the deathly

silence of
childbirth
etching itself in

humans and
animals. I
go mad in

the snow. My
footprints fuel
the mind

of masters.
An insect slashes
through the air and

goes.

THE RIGHT OF THE POWERFUL

The right of the powerful is to take everything.
Memory and youth, clouds and
sadness. I didn't know,
I swear I didn't know what I was doing
when I stole your heart. I was
just happy, touched and grateful to my
bright stars. I thought my quarry
was love, and dust, now mute,
a gift. I bred plenty
of species. Winged monkeys and
blue cockatoos. I even
tempted you, foxes, to become
the king of beasts. I really thought I was
God's ant who carried everything
on its shoulders alone. That's why
I rot and grow delirious for the hour
when you'll turn green, meadows. With
the obliteration of my body, the signet will be
returned to you. Crickets and springs, the sunrise
over Trenta. The soft
mists over home will be holy
again, like they used to be.
Just a moment, poisoned children. Just
one sip before I return
to the earth.

The heart of Europe is elegant and
dead. Only
children tremble before time crushes
them. We are torn by two
larger facets: Satan, the institution
of the front door and the overhang
of freedom, which converge in
the Pacific. But we
are memory. Therefore obligatory
for the world, although our myth is built into
a machine that we no longer have at our disposal.
Our only real historical option is
mercy, the only thing
we truly can no longer
consume or operationalize.
Psychoanalysis is the bottom, the night before
the revelation. All the laboratories of power will
fall.

Whom should we call? The place, the nation is
wiped out. Guns didn't help it,
it was too poorly armed to defend
itself. The enemy grew in the heart,
within. In the hatred toward themselves,
in the hatred of their freedoms,
in hatred—those panics on the stairs,
so characteristic of jobs like this when a storm
is brewing—toward the masters of envy and some
crumbs they initially procured for
the treatment of their dead souls. Bastard without
a name, bastard with his fairgrounds, how
do you want to legitimize yourself to me? Do you think
you're better because I speak a language that
apparently resembles yours? With the first word,
I was right. You've been destroyed from
within, the blood flowed into emptiness. Silence and
deafness are your endeavors, the dull gargle
of strangled children and aborted dreams.
Look, you've been discarded, silently wiped out and
no one even noticed. I still remember
the liberation of Ljubljana, yours and mine—
ours—the nervous smoking of that
Russian on the balcony, the speeches by the poet and
condottiere, lovers of air who then
consumed their internal organs, like before
that Vrhnikan and everyone who couldn't afford
the 60 guilders to pay
for a train to Vienna. In 1910. In
1974. Incompetent, save for filming
liquidations, the ridiculous pellicles of miserable
deaths, fruit fetid from birth, which
will fertilize a rock. What seed? A land without
sea and God. What use is a house to you if it's
dead and empty, the cries of victims you
tortured publicly in collective ecstasy and an exquisite
yearning to be redeemed. Vampire,

bloated anniversary of death, lush subalpine
ear of golden altars. Exactly so.
As in the rural baroque and Chile. I don't even
have as much in common with you as the blackness
under a fingernail does. I'm giving you back the idiom.

FLASHLIGHT

Now I'm standing among
a spruce, which is wrapped in a diaper,
and a larch, which is wrapped in a diaper,
and a fern, which is wrapped in
a miniature diaper. My flashlight
is shining because it's night. I cough.
My cough reaches farther than the light
of the flashlight. I unfasten the diapers from the trunks,
my eyes hurt from the miniature diaper.
I wish a wolf would come and rip me apart.
Someone fragrant walked this path
to the cabin. I turn on the flashlight again
to see where I've come.
Moss is made for resting hands. We sleep
and wake up on the moss.
Baby Jesus is surrounded by sheets
of moss. Not only would I like to be ripped apart
by a wolf, I want to live because I want
to throw a greengage from the corner of the room
into a pool that is a sheet of glass.
But there's no river in the desert!
They'll also domesticate me like that.

SHIPS

I'm religious.
As religious as the wind, or scissors.
An ant eats, she's religious, the flowers are red.
I don't want to die. I don't care if I die now.
I'm more religious than the dust in the desert.
The mouth of a child is round. My eyes are
syrup, dripping cold.
Sometimes I think nettles stung me, but
they didn't. Sometimes I think I'm miserable, but
I'm not.
I'm religious.
I will throw a barrel into the river.
If bees rushed into my face, I'd scratch
at them with my hand and would see
again.
I don't get upset.
The soul presses like the crowds at the door.
When I die, oxen will graze the grass just like this.
Houses will glimmer just like this.

UPBRINGING

I live there, where God wants me.
I have no inherent will, this is
stupidity, to say this is stupidity.
God orders me to all these meetings.
If I have a will, it's like an old wooden fence: rotting.
Or we burn it, yes, burn it.
Sometimes I watch the fire in the chimney for hours and hours.
The fire is my brother.
Sometimes I breathe and nearly scream from madness.
But silently, wordlessly and silently, so that the pleasure is great.
The air is my brother.
But the most terrible brother is my
body, which is myself.
I myself am the brother.
I have many sisters: raindrops.
The sisters drench me.
Now I live in heaven because I put him outside.
I weep because there are people who don't want to live in heaven.
It's harder to find a person than a gold mine.
Sometimes I think, if I drench them, they'd all go to heaven.
And I drench them and they go to heaven, but then they fall out.
People say I cut off their
arms because my arm moved.
People blame me.
I'm suffering because I think I kill.
Sometimes I think everyone killed themselves because of me.
I go to their graves.
They don't resent me.
They consecrate everyone who has killed.
But I'm light, very light.
When I die I'll be even more terrible.
Sins are my allies.
Sometimes I put a scarf on my head.
Then I walk with the scarf on my head like some
tiger in a cage.
When it's time, the chains burst on their own.
And some plane takes me and I go.

Wherever I arrive, I kiss the ground.
Today the pope is imitating me.
But popes are fools, I think only of
Christ.
That's why I don't like sweaters on my skin.
A dead sheep hurts, a dead sheep hurts.
But I'm created differently than Christ.
Sometimes Christ really gets on my nerves.
They buried him in a field.
The field no longer produces ash.
I'm producing ash.
I always drench the bread with tears.
Christ stopped weeping.
If we swam together in the sea, I would dunk him.
Who does the crawl better?
Who's better at diving from the cliffs on Menorca?
That boy who was twenty years younger?
He wasn't developed.
His parents didn't put him in the better schools.
I'm amazed when I come across such
young people who don't know how to swim fast.
This seems to me like a sin of the parents.
I carried him on my shoulders and threw him into
the water to teach him to dive.
Christ also wore a sheep on his head.
But images flooded Christ.
I beat on the frescoes and howl.
I lack composure of spirit.
Even the limbs that he casts aside heal.
Why didn't they eat his flesh when it was still sweet!
When I die, my flesh will be sweet.
And if you won't eat it then, I'll set myself on fire now!
I want you to eat everything I make
even if you vomit after.
I saw people vomiting and
dreaming of killing me.
My friends wanted to cut open my veins.
But all His life God was my
friend, so I escaped.

I'm just waiting for some tragedy.
Tragedies comfort me.
Tragedies open all doors.
And now I callously smoke when I write.
I'm callous and merciless.
My kindness bites through animals' windpipes.
Only monsters are in God.
There are monsters in God because the world is undeveloped.
When you open it, the world bursts just like an egg.
There's always some kind of sperm in my body.
I must see my sperm.
I see such gardens that
the people next to me go crazy.
When they get dizzy in the head and crash,
I know that I'll write.
People are, to me, puppies that bite themselves.
Roses never bite themselves.
Roses are entrenched, I like everything that moves.
A rose moves only when its petal falls.
The petals are falling into my blood!
I'm a rose petal!
A lynx, a lawn, a spider, gold, a clock, death,
a father, a mother, a boy, an old man, a wall, a frog,
a crust of bread, the wind, a whip, the whiteness of the soil,
a spike, a water lily, a wire, an aura, the north, whatever
has cabbage inside its head, a torturer and a martyr,
a blackbird, a bucket, a bridge, a sieve, an apple, bread,
the bread crust I throw away, a head, a signet,
a cylinder, a tree, lightning, a bee, a mountain,
a tiny baby, a slightly larger baby,
dew, a carnival, a balcony, a drum, a power that
washes while it eats.
I'm an everlasting geyser.
I raise them so that they'll write me.

ONLY SNOW REMAINS

I think about God instead of thinking about
snow. That isn't true.
God thinks about me and eats me.
No one thinks about anyone.
A stroller goes down the road.
Snow falls when it falls.
God is a total foreigner, planted by nothing.
I would love to be planted like a willow.
I would love to be planted like grass.
And then I would fall on it like snow, softly.
I would go to sleep and pull back the blanket of God, my
skin, and vanish in the street, into the night.
Yesterday I walked by a door.
A door swinging from knees to chest.
I wanted to go in and see if an angel was inside.
There was an old man with a sombrero.
With dark skin and even darker eyes.
I poured out tequila.
I tipped it back.
And there was no sound like I'd turned on
a faucet so that water flowed.
I must drink the tequila.
I must be a tree, planted in the earth, and open the door.
I must meet the angel.

HOME

Far away, where the meadows are dark.
A dry flower grows, sprinkled with snow.
And a rooster crows even though it's cold.
It walks, its feet are like little hooves.

Far away, where a flower blossoms through the snow.
Blue blossoms on white snow.
The sun embraces it and puts it to sleep.
Love guards it from the cold.

Far away, where waterfalls ricochet off ledges.
Where chamois guard the grass with their bodies.
There's a bridge. I dangle from the bridge.
And I don't know if I'll jump or swim.

Far away, the sound of spoons is coming from a house.
Smoke, white smoke in the clear sky.
It smells of bread. It smells of žganci.
A girl opens a window. So that the little birds may eat.

Far away, in the forest there are colorful ribbons on the spruces.
The spruces are covered in snow, there is no sled.
A ribbon is torn and floats like a kite
so that you may rest your head on the sky's blueness.

TREE OF LIFE

I was born in a field of grain and snapped my fingers.
White chalk crossed the green blackboard.
Dew set me on the ground.
I played with pearls.

I leaned pastures against my ear, and fields.
The stars sizzled.
Under a bridge I carved an inscription: I can't read.
Factories were being washed with salt water.

Cherries were my soldiers.
I tossed gloves into the thorns.
We ate fish with a golden bread knife.
In the chandelier above the table not all the candles were lit.

Mama played the piano.
I climbed on my father's shoulders.
Stepped on white mushrooms, watched clouds of dust.
From the window of the room, I touched the branches.

TOTEMS ON BANK ROOFS

There is no difference between a murderer
and a sip of wine. Delight is stopping
the flow of blood. Let life
wilt on the hand. Let crystals
evaporate. Everyone finds his position,
dead or alive. The poet is a craftsman
who makes social balance possible
for an intangible presence. Souls kneel
in front of a calf first. It also feels
an itching and yearning,
but the calf is placed in warm
soapy water. Every animal has
its bunker. Only we are cathedrals
in which memory doesn't get lost.

GAY BAR

A black vulture crushes my bones.
A white vulture in a photograph.
Houses open their mouths, swallow
flowers. Lightning doesn't choose. I brushed
the spruces by hand. A cart has a tire, a farmhand
a whip, trashcans are falling. We have
two natures. The vulture circles the belfry
at Ptujska Gora. Gingerbread hearts, red
blood, something awaits! Dawn bangs into
the bricks of Brooklyn. I'm still asleep
in silvery milk. When the wind strokes the grass,
I'll be in front of the house. Crickets will burn the air.
The sound will be like in the hall where
there's plush lining in Christ's tomb.

Y

On this side of Manhattan I practiced my
Law. I cleaned the city with my white teeth.
I hung flags to orient myself more easily,
lowered flags to the ground and wrapped corpses in them.
No one discovered the mistake for a while. I wasn't even wrong
about Y. But the soul is eternal, not the letter. One
fine day I ran out of money. It was around
six in the morning when I sat on a bench and everyone else
was still asleep. I had to tear a board from the bench
and make a boat, like when I came here.
I even convinced the guard to release it into
the sea with a pulley. And now I'm paddling and building
my muscles. I know: on this side of Manhattan I will
practice my Law again. The soul is eternal, not the letter.

FUNCTIONS

To desire means to cancel death.
To strike its white skin with a stamp
and then stare at the eggs.
To turn the vase so that it hisses like a top
and to demolish hymns.
In nature there are many surfaces,
one of them walks along the edge and bites milk.
To desire means to collapse in the galleys.
To sizzle the blows.
To spill wine on a tray and wash
your hands with it.
To desire is the engine of the head, not the heart.
The hunger of dried fish, dead in steam boilers.
A strawberry grape falls every minute.
Shoulders widen.
To desire means to strip the black cross from the farmer.
To sing in clearings, to call into the void.
To hit the horns of blood and to beat them, beat them.
Under the sun, where rancor is at home, our discus is rancor.
To desire means to breathe.
To scrape moss from barren parallel bars by hand.
To pant, to pant.
To burn meat, cut it into cubes so that it gets
a black head like a cricket.
Amber is in trees, not people.
To desire means to sleep, to sleep and forget about everything.
Pistons are beautiful.
Hay on a cart is the enemy of the people.
Farmers with long beards sleep in it,
holding pitchforks over their waists.
To desire means not to smoke.
To cross your arms over your chest and think of the Arno.
You were bigger than the Danube.
To desire means to count your brothers, there are plenty of them.
To run at the secret headquarters with your head bowed and shout a cry
of freedom.
Four people on a chair quarter it.

It walks the world like a species and dies out
with dark circles around its loins.
To desire means to fade with ironwood, cane, maple.
To rub snow into your shoulders.
To stand, to wave at trains and wail like those
who are chained by flight.
To desire means to greet a worm and respect it.
To pour liquor there on your knuckles.
To desire means to knock down the sun and crush it like
a snowball in the palm of your hand.
To stack coat upon coat, sheepskin upon
sheepskin, dead.
To snap necks in front of power plants and fall asleep like a flower.
Let it sleep, let it sleep.
Let it wither in a spasm of madness.
Tribes dance in circles on the black wadding of the dead.
Let skin flow over my veins like
banknotes over the blood of the Indians.
To desire means to break up a storm, to scatter
diamonds in coffee.
To seize the dance.
To seize every dancer separately.
To desire means to listen calmly to hail
killing hamsters.
To climb onto a rocking chair and wrap your fingers around all
the toddlers who died like seed.
To grow a shadow.
To grow a shadow like a cloud of riffraff.
To slice the skin of drums.
To fall asleep, to fall asleep.
To desire means to scrape salicylic acid from crowns.
To sink, to sink.
To stare at the ears of people picking grapes and call
them here.
Everyone knows a little, I know a little.
An open palm knows more.
To desire means to scrape time.
Let the servants with a stone in their hand
stitch it up.

Hey, Pythagoras! Brat! Brat! Artemis's white coat was
puked on.
To desire means to twist a bird's head so that it will never
sing again.
To straddle a pillar instead of a window and listen for
distant ignitions.
To desire means that all limbs crash against the rocks.
The cliffs become clear.
The gate curves in front of the field.
God hears only diluted magma, nectar.
To desire means not noticing the last time you put on your
shoe.
To desire means to joke that scorpions
hang on their dazzling
stingers until they're covered in bronze.
To desire means to concede to death.

THE FISH

I'm a carnivore, but a plant.
I'm God and man in one.
I'm a pupa. Humanity grows from me.
I have a perfectly spilled brain, like
a flower, so that I can love more. Sometimes I put
my fingers in it and it's warm. Wicked people
say that other people drown
in it. No. I'm a belly.
I welcome travelers in it.
I have a wife who loves me.
Sometimes I get scared that she loves me
more than I love her and I'm miserable and
depressed. My wife breathes like a little
bird. Her body relaxes me.
My wife is afraid of the other guests.
I tell her no, no, don't be afraid.
All the guests are single and for all of us.
A white match with a blue head has fallen
into my typewriter. My nails are dirty.
Now I'm mulling over what I should write.
One neighbor lives here. Her children make
a lot of noise. I'm God and I calm them down.
At one I'll go to the dentist. Dr. Mena,
Calle Reloj. I'll ring the bell and tell him
to pull out my tooth because I'm in too much pain.
I'm happiest in sleep and when I write.
The masters pass me from hand to hand.
This is necessary. This is as necessary
as for a tree that's growing. A tree needs soil.
I need soil so I don't go insane.
I'll live for four hundred fifty years.
Rebazar Tarzs has already lived for six hundred years.
I don't know if he was in that white coat
because I cannot tell them apart yet. When I write, I have
another bed. Sometimes I flow more like
water because water loves the most.
Fear hurts people. A flower is softest

if you put a palm on it. The flower enjoys
the palm. I enjoy everything. Yesterday I
dreamed that my father bent down to
Harriet. I get scared of other women and
that's why I don't sleep with them. But the distance between
God and young people is small.
In God there's always one woman, and this is
my wife. I'm not afraid that the guests will tear me
apart. I can give them everything, but it still grows back.
The more I give, the more it grows. Then it floats away
to help other creatures. On one planet there's
a collection center for my flesh. I don't know
which one. Whoever drinks from it will be
happy. I'm a tube. I'm God because
I love. I have everything dark here, inside, nothing
outside. I can illuminate any animal.
I'm starving. When I hear the juices in my
body, I know I'm in grace. I'd have
to consume money night and day if I wanted
to build my life, but it still wouldn't
help. I'm made for this,
to shine. Money is death. I go out to the terrace.
From there I see the entire landscape, up to Dolores
Hidalgo. It's warm and soft like in Tuscany,
but it's not Tuscany. I sit there with Metka and
look. The sun sets and we still sit and
look. She has arms like Shakti. I have
a face like an Egyptian animal. Love is
everything. Moses's basket never
crashed on the rocks. Small horses walk
out of the flat landscape. Wind is blowing
from the Sierras. I go into people's mouths head
first and kill them and give birth,
kill and give birth, because I write.

My intelligence is criminal.
My soul is criminal.
My fingers are criminal. My waist.
All that's on me is criminal. From A to Ž.
Edge, handkerchief, shed, shed, sword, sword.
And the dreams of my readers. Criminal.
Only the flowers on people's graves beside my
road smell of the innocent who passed by here.
On foot.

The sky will open.
I was chosen for the continuation
of the world.

A strand—from everyone—
blazing white kisses that
soaked me.
I believe in education.
Light—the material of poetry—
is a miraculous power.

The mystery
of the flower—the people—
alone.

May no one
be afraid of wounds and
the death of my body.

The cabbage—
the heart of the world—is
mine.

Eternity is
cruel and crystal.
It nullifies

the living.
It replaces people and
loves and doesn't

open
the well. You wipe the glass
with a hand,

you don't
break it. Let every
love

die, just like
man. Death
protects us.

SONNET ABOUT MILK

Gentlemen! I found the milk, my bloodthirsty
milk! In a little blue pot on the stove!
These cow trickles poured at the height of my waist,
left of the window, are the basis of all my misfortune.

If I heat it, it boils! If it boils, it overflows!
How to adjust to the white madness!
It hates its own form and is a pot now.
And I look at Daniel, who's building us

a house under the window, and don't notice him!
Today is Friday, the 7th of March. I've already eaten everything.
Cauliflower, soup. There'll be nothing left for

the guests. Absolutely nothing left. When the milk
rises, my shoes squeak on the cement.
I should have changed them a long time ago.

EAGLES

In a bag I have hair, a brush, toothpaste.
Cypresses grow on the hillside.
Cypresses attacked the lice.
The lice fraternized with the sun.

The stones are red and very worn.
If you turn the stone on its stomach, its back is hidden in the soil.
A man with a sombrero opens the door with two sticks.
He'll go after the horse and he'll ride the horse.

Why are all leaves greasy except cypress leaves!
Why does rain wash the blood!
I see workers putting down pavement.
At that time there still was no ceiling in my house.

DIOCESES

I was locked in a bathtub and in fourteen days I wrote a novel.
Weeds grew over the walls, the hills, the swamp.
Father was a wall, mother was a shock on the thighs.
I recognize this, he told me, it's just like in a large theater.
I feel it.
It poured from the rock, it poured, it didn't look like it would stop pouring.
Then I went for a walk. I looked at the roads and palaces, many so old and
    exquisite that only the Romans could have built them.
Allow me, sir, said a bishop, to go to work at once. This is to say, we will
    break down the door to the pavilion, catch the riffraff hiding in it,
    and all this will be finished.

CHRIST

If I swallowed mother, fish would rip her apart
in my throat. That's why I'd prefer nailing her
to a gun. Let her flutter like a flag with wet paws,
is what the boy with the bundle thought before
falling asleep. For a long time he dreamed of nothing,
then suddenly of Christ eating kohlrabi.
Why are you doing that? he asked him. Why
don't you leave the kohlrabi alone? Christ didn't know
what to do because no one had ever reproached him
over greenery before. What should I eat, he said.
Hey, said the boy with the bundle, let's go hunting,
you'll catch a rabbit. And they went.
And the light that streamed from Christ's stomach
grew much weaker, so they started
to stumble over stones. I'm not skilled,
the Lord said, I've never caught
a rabbit. Leave that to me, said the boy
with the bundle, but there's no light. And Christ
ate another kohlrabi and immediately
lit up again. You're swindling me, said the boy.
The light would need to shine anyway.
The rabbit will be just for me if you don't
straighten up. And it was so bright
that the rabbits were like festivals. And one
gave them an eye and another a nose and this
was enough and no one died.

OPUS DEI

Whatever touches me is consecrated.
Certainly! Even if
you lick and crawl under the shower.

Have you ever died without air?
I have.

Have your eyeballs ever been wrapped in
blue paper ribbons?
Mine have.

I munched through all the avenues.
Poured the Forbidden City into myself.

Clean steps, strands of nature
and a caressing sun remain for you.

I returned the measure to man.

FLOWERS' CLOTHING

I saw a flower growing out of the sand.
What does this flower signify?
The flower had a saddle in it.
What does this saddle signify?
As I rode, the saddle fell off.
The sea remained, and on the walls, yellow noodles.
Some were bent, others broke in half,
a shapeless yellow
visible through them.
The water turned bloody.
Leaves started to fall into it.
When I smelled it,
I knew it was laurel.
I felt the ground beneath my toes.
At first the ground was moving.
It seemed like it had a corroded and hard back.
I couldn't remember a turtle having a relief.
The water was drained.
Everything that floated in the water
flew under me.
But there was no ground.
I walked over the vacant hardness.
Far away a long wet broom was sliding across
the horizon, I couldn't see if
it was alive or not, if it was rolling up
legs or fur, or if something was only
hanging from it and it wasn't a broom
at all.
Then we were all sucked into a soft substance,
a boiling mirror, but it didn't burn.
It was boiling only because it was
liquid, not from
heat, and it started to harden.
I was up to my waist in the flower growing out of the sand
and I knew immediately that now I could go
anywhere.

I'm damned.
Flowers wither beside me
because I make love only with God.
A cat washes my paws.
Your command burns.

I don't consume saliva, I consume You,
who gave me life.
Will the heart disperse the clamor?
We'll all die and depart.

The rain erases me.
Will love burn in fire?
Will you behold who you are
without me?

POPPY

Cover up the people when I step into the room.
Throw blankets, tents and powdered milk on them.
Bury them in the soil, I'm a hamster.
Wrap them in gauze.

Draw crosses over their mouths.
There's a fire in the Laurentian Library.
Breathe bread and soil and rain,
choke your children with the bran of oars.

My soul is a dark sleepless agave.
A panther that breaks every cage.
Because when I step over the stars, which are my
work, white dust creaks under me.

SIERRA NEVADA

In my hair is all history, all
bloodred atlases.
My hair drives the universe into a frenzy.
If a flower blossoms, it blossoms only because
it opened up access to my hair.
Granite, purer than the tears of heaven
that drip on Hermes's chest.
And when dogs have babies and
give birth: it's because of my hair.
Rome collapsed when
my hairs got tangled.
In the sun, a view of the Sierras, bees,
and trees and hymns, cast into a zigzag.
Honey scratches my throat: my hair.
Horses change into bundles.
Ha, someone sketched the back of a stone and arranged
the mountains exactly as they stand!
He drew walls in them and spilled air
all over them. The world is a torte.
A heart, frosting and almonds on it.
Hair is more marvelous than alcohol.
Yeti graze together with sheep and
goats and there's a springy
bridge they threw kings from.
I'm rocking.
My hairs are torrents.
Sometimes I connect cupboards with a thin wire
and tie them to a cart.
A train that puffs heavily, like some
pilgrim. *Get it done!* I whisper
blissfully, history gets
more and more fragrant petals.
I attract women because they have less hair.
They're cold, without a man it blows on their head
and children are on the hunt for a father, a real
father, so the one that has hair in
his mouth can devour the thin,

polished strokes of billiard balls,
manna, fluttering their lashes.
I'm hair.
I'm the father of hair.
I'm a chicken thigh on my
sheets that the wilderness breathes on
and with its every breath lures to a flower.

ROBI

Sometimes, at night, when everyone is already asleep
I cry because I know I'll go to hell.
Aunt Liza won't go, and she is fatter than me.
The pillows prick me.
I can't sleep because I think too much.
When I stop crying I turn on the light.
I relax only if I make a bunny hand
that goes on the wall.
I have no friends because I fell
down the stairs when I was three.
They say I was so scared then that I'm coming apart now.
They call me Trashcan.
Dad works all day.
Mom works at the market.
Liza cooks and beats me because she hasn't found a husband.
At school they are all thin.
We have a school whose wall is crumbling.
The fence is all rusted, and if you
grab it you get brown hands.
I always wipe my brown hands in the grass so that
the brown color doesn't get on my pants.
Nobody comes to get me at school anymore.
When I grow up, I'll be alone.
Aunt Liza saves up like a polecat, for a dowry,
and never puts enough on my plate.
I don't eat anything.
Stars must be very light.
Sparrows aren't so light as I thought,
I weighed them.
For as big they are, they're as heavy as me.
If I could fly, I would lose weight.
I know how the air sweeps across my cheeks if the window's open in the car.
Only my legs are normal.
Now I'm saying what I think.
Whoever doesn't say what he thinks falls apart.
Large animals emerge inside him
and press on his belly with their backs.

I sometimes think I'm a box that has
another Robi in it. And in that Robi there's another Robi.
There are three of us and each of us goes in all directions alone.
One day I'll let go of them both.
I'll buy myself a very thin rope and tie them both
by the legs so that they can graze and go their own way.
All day, all night I'll be without them, and if my stomach
shrinks, I'll cut the rope and they'll get lost
in that space, where they'll graze.
And they say: if someone really wants to lose weight,
he shouldn't eat for a week.
But if I left them both outside for a week, they could freeze.
They could get lost.
It isn't certain if I'd be thinner if they didn't exist.
It isn't certain.
And then it would seem like I didn't even have arms.
That's right.
They're my arms and my brother, I have one on each
shoulder, inside, in my body, they're just like
butterfly wings in a pupa.
One day they'll leave.
And then I'll have dried-up arms.
I'll toss the two old arms into hell, go down
the stairs and burn them.
I have no other brothers, because Aldo is blond.
One brother cannot be blond, the other brunette.
I'd like to go to mass alone, not together,
let Aldo crash into the church door, let him
stay there crumpled like a snowball.
Let them all stay there crumpled.
There should be no crowding in church, so that you can see yourself with God.
But this is how people bring the stench from the kitchen into church.
If they wash and dress nicely, it doesn't help, I smell food.
I smell food during the elevation.
I smell food during confession.
They don't let me touch Christ.
Sometimes they let people kiss
his feet, but lately they want to draw him
as if he were a gym teacher, and that's disgusting.

Aunt Liza is the most disgusting because
she's the fattest and that's why she doesn't find a husband.
I'll tear down the fence at school.
And when mom comes home she won't have
those dead eyes anymore.
And dad will read books to me.
The story about the bean.
Why am I the smallest and the fattest?
Why do bunnies also mate?
Couldn't God have made it so that at least
the bunnies are clean, not guilty of anything?
Everything alive, whatever grows, mates, and sin eats
on and on at the edges of deserts.
Shrubs.
Grass.
It even dries up those pools that only Arabs know about.
People mate and their eyes go dark.
From a young age the soul already flows from a person, just like
wine from a bottle held by a drunkard who
cannot find his mouth anymore.
I'm so fat because I hold onto my soul.
I hold onto it for all three.
Robi, Robi, Robi, Trashcan, Lump.
It's better to go to hell with your soul than to go to
heaven if you have to give up everything.
I'll tear down that fence, even if my
pants will then be brown as shit.
The pillows prick me.
They turned off my light.
They say I won't sleep if the light is on, but that's backward.
If the light's on, I calm down because I see my bunny.
If I see the bunny, I can pray for him.
I can pray for every part of the bunny's body,
for his ears, for his little paws, for his gray tummy, for his little eyes,
for him to have little calm bunny eyes.
If I pray like this for a long time and move my hand
quite slowly, my hand becomes the bunny.
Sometimes the bunny is entirely on the wall, sometimes
he's entirely in my hand.

The pillows prick me.
The window must be open and it must be
warm as well.
If you don't suffocate, the window should not be closed,
but the air should not circulate too much either.
Air that circulates too much mates.
Everyone who mates loses their independence.
The air is just as diluted as old sugar
that has no strength anymore.
Air should be constantly fresh, but inside, in the soul.
Air should circulate only in the soul.
I'll cut wounds in myself.
Let a rose grow from my wounds so that
my bunny will have company.
And under the rose let there be a carpet of clover
like there is at the bay at Ankaran.

TO THE HEART

Raucous black sky, why did you swallow
my evidence?
Who authorized you to eat this?
My brothers are flowers.
Do you still smell bundles of hay and lemon blossoms?
Submerging a body in water eliminates the smell.
Allahs smoke pipes on the shore.
Together we burn our eyelashes.
Raucous black sky, did you count the food?
What will you do in a crowd of white cherries?
Is there some wedge in your gluttonous cavity?
What papers are you burning under the pagoda?
Don't birds collide with your eyebrows?
You, who doesn't distinguish the albumen from the yolk,
where do you put the colors?
Do you think I'll feed you like an hourglass
that can be flipped into eternity?
I'll break a horseshoe, we'll see if
you'll keep breathing!
And your gates will burn down beneath
the surface of the water. .
Raucous black sky, my neighbor!
Arrange, arrange the stones!
Let the otters crush eyes on them
so you can smell and count more easily.
You're a belt!
A not-father!
Your parade of clay and silk flags
goes insane at the touch of one another.
So where is the papier-mâché?
Are the stars in my body wounded?
Have you ever asked them something?
You have gods locked in bowls like peasants
in casks stomping on their cabbage.
You're deaf!
I've bitten off your heel five times already!
But it grows back like the beards of saints in

deserts because they eat nothing.
The earth is my bonbon, gluttonous!
We'll divide the remaining fruit in half.
I beat the rug in your mouth, blackened,
so that you'll cough!
And I'll roll my children in fish
bones, bend and glue them to straighten
them out and slit your
throat when you smack your lips and dream
of the heat because you drank my blood.
Raucous black sky, give me back my number!
Do you see those twisted damp paws?
They're for you, if you agree to the rules of the game.
Let melancholy flow like a river for us both!

LAPIS LAZULI

I spent three nights in a row among the gnostics.
White butterflies chased each other above red flowers
and snakes circled and devoured themselves. Here, everything
just like there. People are born and die, we put our hands

on their heads. Only the hair of my friends
there was thicker. Will the human race
lose its hair? And I met lynx who
told me they were from Dacia. And there was no

Mohamed and because of this there was a hole in
the belly of the earth. Wow! Some curves! Lumps of flesh
soaked with spirit and endless ships with white
sails. Are they setting off for oil? And don't believe

that the sects were any kinder to each other.
Communists devoured the monkeys and the monkeys
threw bananas at kings. The hat and the pot
were the same. I remember cooking myself meat

on a stone the first night because I didn't know
I could use my hat for this. Now
it flashed back to me! Our hair lacks grease!
Who else is placing rocks around the trunks! But the water

still babbles when it flows. And the skin still
glows so terribly. And the train that rushes
from the flesh to the heart so that lizards jump off
the rails in a panic and the sky is completely covered

by a scarlet coat . . . No! I say. It's blue! And I roll
from my back to my belly and shoot at
the sky. And the earth, the faces, the loves that passed
through my life, all of it becomes lapis lazuli.

DEATH'S WINDOW

To stop the blood of flowers and reverse the layers.
To die in the river, to die in the river.
To hear the heart of a rat. There is no difference
between the silver of the moon and the silver of my tribe.

To clear the field and run to the edge of the earth.
To bear a crystal in the chest: the word. Soap
evaporates at the door, fire illuminates the day.
To look back, to look back one more time.

And to remove the robe. The poppy has bitten the sky.
To walk empty roads and drink shadows.
To feel the oak at the mouth of the well.

To stop the blood of flowers, to stop the blood of flowers.
Altars watch each other face to face.
To lie down on a blue cabbage.

FIELDS OF ZINC

Do you think someone will come?
Do you think I'll hear them sing?
Do you think I'll have a bloody hand?
I've been hired to murmur.

We murmur, we murmur,
put our legs over the pipe,
love ourselves, love ourselves,
and at the same time swim with spring.

Do you think the lion will betray him?
How would it betray him if it can't sit?
Do you think they're unloaded?
We lock the steam in the cellar.

We murmur, we murmur,
put our legs over the pipe,
love ourselves, love ourselves,
and at the same time swim with spring.

SUTRA

What is the sea? The sea is a forehead.
What is a forehead? A forehead is night.
What is sand? Sand is the dawn.
What is the dawn? The dawn is a king.
A king is a clothed man.
A clothed man bears a burden.

What is a bag? A bag is trash.
What is trash? Trash is a wheel.
What is color? Color is gas.
What is gas? Gas is a child.
A child embraces the Bible.
Break his Bible.

What is to bear? To bear is delight.
What is delight? Delight is Bach.
What is wisdom? Wisdom is silence.
What is silence? Silence is the four.
The four, crossed and circled.
The world is a boot stirrup.

MY TRIBE

My tribe
no longer hears
freedom.

Doesn't recognize it,
doesn't see it
when touched by it.

My tribe
thinks
that the slow

killing
of their bodies
and souls

is natural.
But sometimes
when some ozone

resembling
childhood
invades it

for a moment,
it wipes its sweaty
forehead,

shakes
this nightmare,
these chains

off itself,
rolls over
and falls asleep.

SHEPHERD

The trees were covered with snow, covered with snow.
I warm my numb hands by the fire under the pen.
My sheep collapse from the cold, onto their backs,
they bleat with their milky cries, on their backs.

I've been in the mountains for ages, to guard the Seven
Lakes. How the buzzards circled, hungry, and slaughtered
my sheep one after the other under the Cross!

My soot turned white under the black-blue
arch. Snow and ice consume everything. Everyone
had their time, except me. My delights,

my whistling, my valley. I was always alone
with my cruel dog, who bites the strap of my
bag to get warm from hunger. To stop
the mute sinking of the sheep in the soft snow.

I PROMISE YOU

You broke me like bread.
You eat me like a bird.
I'm on the cross.
I feel like I'm on the cross.

The hour when I'll die for you
grows like a drop of salt.

I'm the sea that will return to you.
I'll water, forge, and define you.
You, too, will gargle from pain
and sweetness. You, too.

Don't be afraid.
All the wounds are yours.
There is no exit.
We fall together into seriousness and delight.

You, too, won't be able
to count to five.
You, too, destroyed by
mystery and fortune.

PONT NEUF

You are my flower, my mouth, my heaven.
In your gaze seven grains are speechless.
I carry them until I collapse.
Until another scent floods the staircase.

You are my pulse, my breath, my grass.
The gentlest criminal, red velvet.
The labyrinth's window will crush you. My palm
systematically gathers you as a glass does color.

We live for murder. The Seine hatches rotten fruit.
And when I lean you against the wall and look around
to see if someone's coming, you retreat into the crystal.
Like a traitor, you prolong my life.

TO READ: TO LOVE

When I read you, I float. Like a teddy bear with paws
you shove me into bliss. You lie on me, whom you
demolished. At death I grew fond of you, first among
the born. In a single moment I became your bonfire.

I'm as safe as I've ever been. You are the ultimate
feeling of satisfaction: to know where yearning is from.
I'm in you as in a soft grave. You carve and ignite
all the layers. Time catches fire and vanishes, I hear hymns

when I look at you. You are stern and demanding, tangible. And
I cannot speak. I know that I yearn for you, hard gray
steel. I'd give everything for one touch from you. Look, the late sun

bangs into the walls of the courtyard in Urbino. I died for you.
I sense you and want you. You torment me. Uproot and cauterize me,
forever. And into the spaces you've destroyed, paradise flows.

BLUE VAULT

With your quiet, slender hand you switch off the stars.
You give away my name like a bee does honey.
Bite me! Scorch my eyes. A distant
sea of buffalo in the ashen, green
air. The taste is replaceable, I'm not.
I am nailed to the cross and I consume your
fruit. Look: every drop of my
memory is a pulse of the arch, still
solidified in the miracle that the sky lives.
An animal succumbs, kneels, is struck.
You shake off the white puffs of the lights and
the inscription on your chest glows for
no one. In your quiet, soft
mouth, you scorched my neck.

GOLEM

You're preoccupied.
You came to see me.
I'm like an olive branch, your face.
Houses blaze in the sun.
The bridge is stuck together stone by stone
and the sky bites.
Hands claim me.
I hear the movement of soft tips.
I'm smoked.
I evaporate into you and savor
your fruit, pedestrian.
A sheep scratching itself against a rock,
the windows are rubbed in sleep.
I'm spilled by sweet training.
I'm twisting your bolts.
I'm seizing the black, silken
chamber of your warm breath,
the temporariness of your life.

BRIGHTLY INSCRIBED IN A NAME

I.

Fuck Šalamun and chain him to himself.
Broken, killed, then just discarded. Let him
entertain his crickets. My flesh tears down the castle
of his mass. Let him be my dog, my madly

enamored Swabian. Let him crawl. Let him
crawl. Let his muzzle lick salt, I command
him. Let him cool down in the name of hatred.
Let his shadow wither first, before he crumbles

alone. Let him leave this world without a drop of water.
Let his entire entourage get my sword in their stomach.
Let all his monsters gargle their

last breath and let them propagate only like
my fathers, my vases from now on. I'll distort
his entire orbit. My program is delight.

II.

I hear your voice, my blood breaks.
I worship through thorns, the subconscious,
through reverence and the wound. My knees
are smashed, they hurt, all scratched up, like

when I was a little boy. I vanish
into your eyes like a siphon. I slice your
white fat. Burn! A bridge has no legs,
no divine peace. Let it crash,

let it crash. Let it blow you up like
a body in the air in the Spanish Civil
War. When limbs trickled like

gobs of blood. Among organs. Shrapnel
gets in your salad. And when the whiteness
bursts, oil is poured over your bones.

RING THE BELL!

You boil that amount of time between.
The difference between when you come and when
you say you'll come. No. It's not
that simple. I'm also not a novice.

The difference between the expected and the actual
arrival, regardless of what you told me.
The Bible must not be read literally. Belts
of spoken time slip away. But in that

new thin strip, new shock of time,
I writhe and wheeze, flooded by yearning, banging
my head against the wall, the floor, or I burn, I burn
folded up in an armchair. With body and spirit

I experience the sweetness of all the anguished before me
or I lie on the bed being torn apart. Saints
were always exterminated in strange ways.
Mankind has always been licked by God.

I AND YOU

Your mouth didn't kiss me, you never
drank snow. You, a melancholy monument now
freezing under an avalanche. I'm asking you a question,
cruelly: are you still warming your igloo? I bewitched you

and tore off your limbs. And the wrinkles deepening
in your once divine forehead, maybe you no longer have
the right to them. You didn't hurt me anymore, you didn't. O little
mummy, aborted flower, the memory of you is disappearing.

There are oceans between us, and you blasé. Hopeless hard
stone, coated with silicate. We'll still make love,
I'll still smear these beehives. My desire is no longer

strong, you won, you're truly empty. And in me,
avenues of countless others, your red heart
is also numb. Only in you did I gurgle from happiness.

THE DEER

The most terrible rock, white white wish.
Water, which springs from blood.
Let my form narrow, let it crush my body
so that all will be in one: cinders, skeletons, a handful.

You drink me as if drawing out the color of my soul.
You guzzle me, a gnat in a little boat.
I have a smudged head, I sense how
mountains were made, how stars were born.

You snatched your summit from me, I stand there.
Look, in the air. In you, who's now poured out and
mine. Golden roofs curve under us,

the pagoda's leaves. I'm in huge silky bonbons,
tender and resilient. I push your mist into the breeze,
the breeze into the divine head in my garden, the deer.

BREAD

If you resist the Door, you'll resist the Pear, too.
The juice, white dust will put you to sleep.
Airplanes roar, blue hellebores spurt. I live in
the warm loaf. The soul is a mushroom in cellophane,

the window is a window, the source of night. Blood gushes,
the vein throbs, fruit falls onto the roof, into the water.
Birds are circling. The river crawls on its knees in
bitter, brown, greasy water. It sees nothing.

It sees a piece of charred meat. Svarun sings
far away. Fur is drying on meters of logs.
Do you have a jug around your neck again?

Your limbs are being twisted, anointed.
I want to say hello, to kiss.
Will you wash your hands when you get on the train?

SILHOUETTE AND ETERNITY

Alliance with death. Pisces with Cancer.
White mouth. The ring, the ring glows.
Spikes. Stakes. A mace.
The groans of the crowd. A quiet run in silence.

Grains fall in a spurt and carry away the chaff.
The nativity is watered. The nativity is watered.
The soft stretched edge is watered.
Colors that include dense forms.

That caress, caress, soften and subdue.
Every link, every plank connects.
The past thunders dully, bursts

into the granary. The grain is at home. The work
is stroking. Quivering. A gift.
Honey. And not a drop is still flowing.

TO METKA

If I burn the white plank of the house, will the flame
be brighter than the weight that falls from our bodies?
Brighter than the samba? Brighter than your juicy head?
I'm in the white snow. You're dancing. Under the colossal

green trees with your juicy sad eyes.
We listen to the rhymes and slips of your brush. Meadows
from which you see moss and what's beneath the moss.
A white lynx scratches in the dark green throat.

Does the sky ever clog and rustle? Where do you rest?
In an avalanche or on the ground? Here I feast, feast,
overeat so that I'm not torn apart in the heights by the pink,

blue and violet clouds and flowers
like Tiepolo, for whom the air washes itself,
before the light floods and crushes us.

RAIN AND HONEY APPLES

The strategic point of the position of maximum pleasure
isn't in a bullet-ridden heaven, secured by
galvanized and intertwined wires.
Mon amour fou lies in the sand, in a shell,

in the mud, and moans like a tired, weary
chatterbox. The masses know his melancholy.
I trample on his death. I attach it.
When it climbs over the edge, I move

the board that has mouse skin attached.
We killed them. On the knots. Now rotten
stumps that memory sizzles with the white
warmth of an exhausted aura. Death waits

for you in a vein. Go somewhere else, Hamlet!
Gold will bury you before you bare your chest.

OXYGEN

Pitching and casting bombs at the nape of the neck is
violent and passionate, the person in question remains
headless. The body turns yellow. Hermes has it,
some other torso doesn't have it. Pitching

and casting bombs into the stomach pulls back a curtain
of water, puppets appear on the stage. A spirit
only smells like this if it burns. Such is
the monument in Rotterdam. When I found

ants in the forest, their metropolis, I
stretched out in my mind and filled up with
air. Became dizzy and crashed on a hill of

needles. I collected all the cyclamen. The drawers
in mother earth rattle and ring at
three. The ants restore order in an instant.

UNTIL THE NIGHT GLAZES YOU

The deadly, dark tone of paradise does and does not resemble
a seabed. It arrives more porously, more
inaudibly, more raspily. You can fall out of the night.

From the black corner of paradise you can fall nowhere.
It crushes you as you would crush lungs. It moves
you before you can even see it. Because knowledge is

in possession. In the forest, wanderers are knocked down into dry
leaves (or into moist ones or into stones) by sandbags,
which fall systematically like the foot of God or

boxing gloves and don't splash, the blows are
blunt, the skin splits but it doesn't splash. The cupboards
are coarse. Glaciers have claws wrapped around

them so that they can welcome a lizard
as with special light effects, it leans,
places its head on the ice. You may have saved

the rails, the switch may have helped a bit,
for a moment you held back the weight
of too large a load gliding centrifugally

around a huge moist belly from the inside, and
when it's used up, free of charge, you will shoot
like a bullet from the belly of all that we know.

WALK

My stone is ribs. They flatten themselves and breathe.
He takes me in his mouth and prays for me. The Lord
will douse me. He'll wet your sugary heart,
see you, brush you. Like a horse, like
a filly. O, my sugary colossus, the heart in
You. Do you hear how drunken hair throbs in
the lobby? Look: it roars from the choir, but you
greedily smack your lips in hardware. I vetoed you.
I'm protecting you. You skip the quiet fragrant
walks when the spruces begin to awaken. You walk
over the Sava with a puppy and breathe and think and are
liberated and free. Carcasses of divine flesh stream down
your throat and you clean them. Thank you.

WINDOWS

Do you remember when I called you
from Chartres? Demoralized and ravenous,
terrible in my desire. You liked dashing from

a dream for the phone and mumbling no, no,
you didn't wake me since I was already jerking off.
But it wasn't true. Even in sleep you occupy an entire

field, the front lines. Then you just concede,
yield in an instant if I attract saliva and
yearning. The scouts in front of the cathedral

started to swarm a little. Both hands were
dying. In the valley (a natural amphitheater)
no whip is cracking. The Franks boiled.

I thought I'd break the window of the cell
with my head and then go on foot, slowly, down
to the cafe. They were all at work. I

smoked. The skittles transformed into
wasps, which marched along the gray velvet
and read from old liturgical books.

PHOTO WITH A YAZOO QUOTE
DEEP IN EACH OTHER'S DREAM

Christ is my sex object, therefore
I'm not ethically problematic. I force
him into meadows. I pasture him, like a little shepherd.

I pick his lice and glands. Will we
rinse off under the tree? When we both lie with
our backs on the ground and look at the sky,

what moves? Will there be enough heat
for winter? Will we peel potatoes? Will we
cast soldiers from lead? And we'll go

to the cows with a hand in their mouths,
we'll nibble horsetail. They looked at Nanos.
Hid in the moss, covered with glass.

When you photographed the tree, did you see to
the blast? What do you mean by this? That
white milk travels through veins into

eternity and glazes the darkness? I'm
a pebble that fell into your flesh.
Flinched you and bound you. We crucified you.

LACQUER

Destiny rolls me. Sometimes like an egg. Sometimes
it stomps me on the shore with its paws. I scream. Struggle.
I pledge all my juice. I must not do this.
Destiny can extinguish me, I've already felt it. If

destiny doesn't blow on our soul, we freeze in an instant.
I spent days in a terrible fear that the sun
wouldn't slip away anymore. That this is my last day.
I felt how the light slid from my hands, and if

I didn't have enough quarters in my pocket and Metka's
voice wasn't gentle and kind and concrete and real
enough, my soul would escape from my body, as it will

someday. You must be kind with death. Everything
is together in a moist dumpling. Home is where we're from.
We're alive only for an instant. Until the lacquer dries.

KISS THE EYES OF PEACE

Kiss the eyes of Peace, which should spill over
the trees. The sun shines outside and no longer roars
so intolerably. The soul hopes to feel its ribs,
its juice again. The cold agreed with me. If
the wind blows and I walk and look at cars, life
returns me to myself. It would be most
terrible because I'd recognize no one when leaving.
They would be too far away to touch or feel.
I wouldn't keep the memory of love in the black
darkness. A crust of ice forms over boiling lava.
Gradually, I might be able to slide again. Walk
along dusty roads. Shake off my jacket if it's
dusty. There was too much honey and grace, that's
all. A person explodes from too much luxury.

BETTER DRUNK THAN OLD

Look, how nicely you combed your hair. Leaf
rites flash in nobility. Pleasure
is in merriment. Tautologies are no longer for

punishment. There's a bead, as if you're creating children.
They're taken from what was already there.
A mountain grows from love, hills grow

from a snake. And if more millipedes grow, a feast
for the eyes is automatic. They flash
without being polished. Hammers, sofas,

worms, hikers on Nanos, why doesn't
air also crash against the air? It
does. The world of the new millennium will be fruitful

and serene. We get accustomed to pleasure slowly
so that it doesn't break us. Look: a pin and
an elephant, my sand in a cup and the Gobi

desert, these are also the distances and magnitudes
between love and love. The body must
adjust to it. We already know what is eternal.

But we must learn what we can take
with us. Young people still have
hope glued to a tassel. They rarely

even know what they have under the birch.
We will dissolve Chinese foot binding,
there will be no return to the dark

throat. Mercy will be infinite and delicious
and divisible and indivisible, and what
was given once will become an incombustible well.

SHEEP, CHAMOIS

You forget the flowers you don't hear. Sweet milk
drips on you. You become melancholic,
despondent. Brutal and disinterested.

Let's beat rocks. Twilight is in the yard.
Chamois, if you jump, fine, do you really think
I'll throw gauze and bandages from the edge of the cliff?

They wouldn't even fall to the bottom. They'd unravel
and be used up in the air. But you think
I'll step down and arch them onto round

stones. The chamois jumps. I don't want to move
you. Protect yourself from the rubble beneath my
feet. It learns from plants. From women

who paint their eyelids. What are all these imitation
blankets, splendid for an organism! The sheep are
installed. The blood of a lamb in plastic

might be used more carefully, like if
you tear off a limb while still alive, she howls. What
may limp with the holy trinity of legs? In the city

we don't peck. A pigeon sleeps in a cramped
basket. And a locomotive, if you put it
on the golden floor of the nave in church, recalls

knights who clattered with their spurs.
The page should always be tall enough so
you can bend over in the saddle and whisper

to him. This is what I want to tell you.
Begin, drill, you'll come across a fresco.
If all the colors aren't there, a trace of colors will be, if

a trace of colors isn't there, the memory of them will be.
You water your life. Ice is made
alone. Alone, it melts with your breathing.

THE CHOPPED SMELL OF MILLS

At night the boiling sun strips. The pole barely
supports the flag. The wind is invisible, juicy, the membrane
of lightning. Every heartbeat propels the head.

The trains are derailed. Glory is from daisies
and tests. In the afternoon I stretched out my arm. The rail
on the bridge was made of hoarfrost. Pebbles roll

under the velvet. The ticking of gravel on the road. The Lapiths
wipe themselves. The grapes don't ripen. A car leaks. Did
Kublai Khan see everything? Did he remember who

whispered? With steam on the blanket. From the blanket on the head.
The axles aren't sealed. Freak out! Not for long
or I don't know how long. By the kilo of horns on

the riverbank, we notice the sun in the dew on the lettuce.
Your gloves are too small. Eyes unsteady.
To start the snow-white shouts. They're in cellophane.

Still! What's arranged by the wilderness and with a fist on dark
nights burns in the mouth. Trumpets blew
with a palm on the stopper. *Vade mecum.* Be salty.

MAMMA MERDA

Geniuses are nasty, monotonous, terrible, and they
remind me of a turtle's jaw.
Shits are for people.
Shit is kind if you excrete it.
It gawks and worries about nothing.
It's smoking like some pig.
It reminds me of the white heights of amber mountains.
Of Gregorčič, for example, specifically
of me and the bloody Soča.
This can be justified to me only by divine frenzy.
That is, divine frenzy is a democratic
institution, the property of all, mostly
children and four-year-old cousins.
They arrive together at family celebrations and say
shit and are already overcome by divine joy,
they shake and roll from happiness and
divine rapture and you say sorry! this isn't
fair, I'm the father, the parent,
I made meat instead of having fun
with them and if I enter the role of my
son, I supplant him, and so I'm backed against the wall.
You're blameless as long as you're
untouchable, that's why it's better
not to linger around those blotting
papers that surround you—
shit is my brother, sin is terrible—
with sons.

TONGUE

You're a jewel made from my power, I eat you like
an ice cube. You pull my arms out of my shoulders and
load them like firewood. You multiply them. I'm ravaged.
My idol was smashed. You're my clay,
my tongue, spit on a clenched fist. And you must
cut me so that my blood isn't strangled by
your seed. Look, I put my fist in a cow's mouth and
scatter daisies around the pool. You're gray, damp
and misty when I stare at the cliffs on the shore of
the lake. Do you know what your belly's like from the inside?
It's like scrubbing your white coated tongue
with the back of your hand when you were still a child.
I want you to buckle from love and even
hit your head a little. I want you to faint.

SHIRT

To tear a shirt and cleanse the soul is essential,
what makes language is accidental.
To burn Joanna Darško.
Jeanne d'Arc has a beak.
A rake stung the bees.
There were no power plants then.
The waters streamed freely.
Fields, impenetrable masses of soldiers, spears.
Meister Eckhart uses the word
distant exactly like a Ljubljana
teenager uses *far out*.
I'd lick them both out of freedom.
I'm licking them both out of freedom.
They just point with a finger: there!
And there it chokes, uproots, and God produces a waterfall over your head.
You lean a ladder against the air and it doesn't fall.
You pump air with pins.
The earthworm is gifted.
It went into the ear hairs.
Where it's wrapped around the trunk
like the tree in paradise around the Serpent.

HALOZE

The otter acts like he ate Boccaccio.
You combined his coats.
One was heard amid the creaking of gulls,
he was called Captain Beef.
He reminded me of Pirjevec.
A wizard's cap, a coat lined with violet
silk, a sewn-on quarter moon and stars.
The sun will rub him.
The whiteness will fry him.
Is the quarter moon like the little mothballs
that no one takes out of the drawer?
And why shouldn't gulls fly downward
from above in a straight line like when
a diamond cuts glass? And why shouldn't
a lighthouse be the kind owned by people, giants
who could just as well munch leaves above
the Loire? Their Cyclopean eye
would throb and flow.
Goya drives leaves into their mouths.
Everything is brown. I sink into
the clay, into the prickly coats of chestnuts,
I'm cold. Is autumn that early?
It flocks and fills the mouth.
They tested the addition by
sending a bull to dance on it. That's why
there are huge bulls by the highways in Spain.

FISH PEACOCK

With juice in the muscles.
I'm not weak, I'm used to it and calm.
I'm melting my eyes.
I hear how the sail flutters.
The sun kisses the white canvas
thirty times and settles
like a blazing club.
What do I care about gusts!
From left and right—the sea!
At first a quadruped uses all
four legs running across the earth.
A bush scrapes, how it tramples, now this, now
that, but what steps into silk,
a crack in the glue, still on the earth?
Is it still in triumph and juice when it lifts off?

In heaven nothing scratches you.
You can't bend your hoof,
there's no granite cube behind your
head. The limbs, rotten, make sense.
The air is gray-bronze,
someone is burning flaxen cloths,
the sheep are drunk and stunned.

You seize the lungs,
they roll over and discover
a fresh cherry pie, which someone
unwrapped before it was put in
a baking dish. Plants grow
inside and outside,
the skin is molded like the moon.

Do you remember the blue underpants and
the record for the hundred-meter freestyle?
How you slumped over the rope.
And your resting pulse,
a bit like a fish that twitches and
a bit like one fanning itself.

MANNA

In the sea there's a dormant
hut, a head sprinkled with
leaves. The hands are

solid,
the skin on them taut like
silk. I see hair in

the glass, as well as
a knee and
a ficus, a plant whose

time
is numbered. Lightness must
fall for you

to become
aware of it. And when
it falls and comes to a stop,

the tissue lovingly
accepts it, the light of the hair
rages.

MEMORY TEARS OFF AN ARM

No diary. No wires. No splashing.
When you take a baby from the bath, he looks,
he isn't bathing, do you wrap his body in

a light gray green towel, or do you just
dab it? It's not good to think. Whales are opening
their planners in the Atlantic. Are they bandaging

feet, skin, veins? There was no glass.
Before there was glass, there was alabaster.
Saints formed a line as if under

some soap. The sky must have
wheezed. It broke through the clouds
on the third fifth of the bridge to Vendée.

Not only. In the shape of the sun. Not like the sun.
Like its light. And still it only
ricochets, glimmering on the skin above

the surface of the Loire, on the space that's
flared up. It's separated from the first and
second and also from the seventh, eighth

and ninth supports. I saw it and
typed it out. As if I were playing with reins.
As if I were supporting the achievement of late

twentieth-century technologies—diagonally—
hiding diamonds, cranberries, accustomed
to how to awaken the horse of the golden

chariot from my eyes facing east.
No one scattered peas on steamships.
The light flares up only when it wants.

WAR

First there's ice. Then pine forests.
Then ice again. Human lives are
wisps. Lines of refugees, houses in flames,

cries like the scratching of colors onto the skin
of salamanders for millions of years. I want to have a yellow
spot. The sun is dislocated now. We think

a lot about what our paws are. Spokes
that the grain stretches around? Red dust
is enough. A little sulfate is enough. And that

smoothness on the porcelain, is it solid? The sediment
of coffee, as if giants were pouring it from buckets.
Odessa stands here. The hunting dogs are here. A crown

inserted in the chest of time. The secularized
version is how a chicken is turned
on the grill. The windowpane lets no heat in. Who

made it transparent? Whose energy is it that
crunches under the teeth? Have you ever spilled a bucket
in the desert? Like throwing snow to chickens.

ATLAS

The flame hoots in my hands. The stem aligns itself.
I plough and weld. A lily rushes like a tram around
my head at the same time as the thorns. Could the handle

disturb Christ? Could you define one
milligram? No, but it pulled you up like
teeth. Like the teeth of a device that hauls the tram.

At the beginning of the century, a lift was built
in Lisbon. In Opčine everything was already there. Somewhere,
the bora is blowing. Somewhere, you drink Fada and stare

at the sea. Here there are people, as if I were sitting
on them. No Fada, no bora. Just us
with Christian, who is entirely torn from

his name. He becomes undeniable. He rolls up his sleeves.
Soon he will start to thrash me alone. The spirit reinforces
our permanence and smells real fighters. In

Provence, they allegedly flirted with Aleš,
and at a key moment in history, they both
blurted out the same thing, which I won't reveal.

CAMUS

The front of the house. This is the large front
of the house. Flight is restrained. Will it navigate
the dust beneath the skin? Hold on to
the human voice. The vault for a trunk of meat. Hold
on to the human voice. It climbs on its nails
pessimistically and grabs a nun. Kiss
Descartes, the one you hate. Slather penicillin
around the fingers. Like the cactus of a hiking boot. Like
a white elephant moving forward. Don't rip up
the roots. Plead for modesty and silence and
earthiness. A strap. You're my strap.
You barely hold on. I can barely resist
the urge to tear you apart completely. Soak yourself
with gasoline and fire. Go into Marshal Tito's
barracks, to the hallway where you kept guard,
into the washroom that you frequented—
a pig trough all around—
where you poured gasoline, lit
a match, watched how the fire burst
into the quadrangle so that you'd calm down.

THE SHINY SLOVENIAN GREEN

To step into the splash. To be adorned. I stepped
over the karst valleys and bloomed. It's plastic
and juicy underground. Whales dive
a little, dart a little. Chile is dewy, spring
is fastened. Girded like an ant, like
a cadet with clay. What do you mean? Beaten like
an icon? Blown up by a small and a large candle?
Slices are also in the trunk, there, where there are
squirrels and hornets lay their eggs. Caesar walks
staccato. Rome crawls at your feet. Anywhere
he plucks a grape, he gurgles. The Irish saved Europe.
They stacked sagas at fire sites. Everything to the north
(Styria). There, in the forests, live charcoal burners with
flashing eyes. They snack on the Book of Kells.

THE MAN I ADMIRED

When I returned from Mexico, I was like
death. My mouth had collapsed and
decayed. I was paying the penalty
for my sins, my palate had dissolved.
I could touch my brain directly
with my tongue. It was painful, terrible and
sweet. When Svetozar was sitting outside
in the waiting room, I knocked down the instrument case.
No, I'm not being precise, he left the office
before me, I only guessed who he was,
I didn't even know him. When I sat down
in the chair, my energy knocked down the instrument
case. To cross from world to world
means an earthquake. Yesterday he died.

NEW YORK–MONTREAL TRAIN, 24.1.1974

At first I was trembling like a switch on water
because of "the chain of accidents." Another thought
was that I wanted to be as systematic

as Swedenborg was. Was the framework clear
and did I accept it even though all the zones of my body
hadn't gone through the groove yet? Right away—

I saw it in a flash—angels are censorship and
fog, just a field of space that pulls you into
the middle. They quickly faded and stuck together

in a lump. I felt physical hands
gently grabbing me under the armpits. The air
buzzed, but not as if a hard body were going

through it, it was like someone was dragging me
through milk. Everyone was expecting me, though
they noticed my physical presence only

gradually: first the old, then those
middle-aged, then the young. As if someone with
a rheostat had widened their field of vision.

Some told me (let it be known)
that they were carrots and that the skin was already
scraped off them in the soil. Some had

only a clear feeling that they must go headfirst through
the waterfall. I wondered what selection brought
them here, but this thought died down because

they stopped it and I couldn't express it.
It was like stopping a drop that
falls into water and then spreads in circles.

Clear waves, I traveled with them.
A compact lump (above my head)
licked me and flooded me with emotion and

delight. A strand (a cone) coming from
this lump pulled me apart,
spread me horizontally, although I was the same.

I knew: they have other sources, infinitely
more powerful, infinitely more peaceful.
I noticed an apparent affinity in clothing.

Veils (clouds) at chest height. I didn't walk
on the ground, but on something suspended, similar
to ice or glass (optically), although I sensed everything:

the moss, the parquet, the grass, the asphalt (green!).
I didn't see this with eyes but with skin, as if
the skin were looking. At the same time I read *Haiku*, I. G.

Plamen, and for a while *The Village Voice*. I was on
the train and looked through the window, read again. In an instant
I understood everything. Language is "articulated" and "mute"

at the same time, occurring in tepid flashes. Accidents
are the humus. As if ping pong balls are flying
from all directions at once and massaging you.

THE DEAD

Or maybe not.
Perhaps their trumpets bend.
They forgot doorknobs during the floods and now
dive for them.
Maybe they're pushing buttons
to cancel the aberrations.
Maybe they're using crepe paper.
Maybe they're not untalented at all and
crackle underwater like shells and
stones, so that every thousand years
the crackling produces for us
a tiny white stone.

ENAMEL

Language doesn't commit itself. It's a purifier and a puritan,
the marbled smooth skin of refined women,
a cork, a self-satisfied little lump. When
Alexander burns down Persepolis, he can
meditate. He dismantles lions in battle like
silky little onions (diminutives strengthen,
inundate), the kindness is harsher than
with Christ, who wishes us all well.
Am I a cold fish that kills Christ with
its tail? Saws through the cross? Should he fall
to his knees again even though he's still riddled
with nails? How will we do this, take him off
the cross so that his knees will bend?
What if they're already cold and stiff, like
the body of Cleitus, whom Alexander
crushed from remorse because he burned down
Persepolis? Clearly, Persepolis had to be
burned down. To denationalize the Rothschilds.

MARCO POLO BROUGHT PASTA

The surface of the pond, rock, spruce. It's late
August, cold for these places. They drove
from Trieste, the cows were given water. There behind
the mountain, on the other side of Vremščica, is
a valley and a river and a mill. Do you also push
the little shovels' moss with your forehead? Water turns
into clay. From clay, gods with swollen
bellies take shape. Then they fall
flat like Chinese soldiers. They roll from
sleep into the grass. The horses lie on their sides.
The left thigh is bloody. The mammoth, the prostitute,
preserved under the ice two thousand miles
further north, weakened the Great Wall
of China. Archaeologists found jam in jugs.

THE DEATH OF FRANK O'HARA

Summer strikes from the clearings. Arrows
are flattened. Copts give out tissues.
Everything is still asleep. The cupboard door fell

down. The lotus sizzles. In skillets, not on
tongues. Did you skip the second floor
in the paternoster? Ride, clamber

out, ride again? Did you wrap the Pope
in violet ribbons? Mice went to the start.
Neighbors take turns. Five vents are in the gray

wall. Like medicinal sod. A marble
falls in warning. No one has opened the taps
yet. Someone steps on the stairs.

He left the bathrobe to lie on the bed.
Someone wavers on whether to complain. Knots
rise up. Oppressed nations need

curtains. The sea evaporates. And when
the hand transforms, it rotates ninety
degrees. When we charged outside,

the maquis had already taken off. Iva said:
Jamnicki. I remembered: grandmothers,
pianos, three sisters, and a brother. My

uniforms, which reeked of horses.
Both Osti and I are from a good house.
Classmates also wear the skins of their children.

The eyes have hazy generations. You
walk the shore and here and there you step on
a small dead whale. Its skin is

cracked. No one else knows. Birds are
eating it now. Brad Gooch sketched
the spot where they covered you with a cloth.

TOMAŽ ŠALAMUN

He's raising a dog in the garden. It ran away from his shadow long ago.
At night he raises rosehip. Entire stairs, rosehip logs.
The rosehip is pruned so that it doesn't crowd.

He tosses his cap into the night. Rosehip is used for lipstick
and, sometimes, sideways for a train. Mystagogues
hauled it out of caves. When he whispers and pants, a boot

comes into the room. Of course, I'm going from the beaks
to the cable car. Prey that weeps loses credit.
The wheel of fortune splits the ping pong ball.

Everyone who bruises a layer of the sky whitewashes a house.
Whoever limps causes a wound.
I know he doesn't even like a teaspoon in a backpack.

Persiflages and barons once went for brushwood.
A cat was struck outside the forest. Father had a white and
yellow one, but as a replacement. A painful sound comes from the deer.

But where do they go between stories?
To sleep in a hotel?
And with whom?

I wouldn't even sail sea foam.
Fruit unnerves me too much.
When we reached Corcovado, a boy

launched a plane into the treetops.
One in Santa Teresa had already stuck posh dolls
in the tram. I gave Rodrigo a cigarette, but

Blažka was in charge. She took us away.
We walked up the hill. I was sacrificed.
And when the garage door closed, we all remained

whole. Gorge on all your books and stop.
Is there meat in the neck?
Even a little circle doesn't inspect a gift.

Dig the pit so that it'll grow.
Frogs are inhuman.
I want my sugar to flow like on a cable car.

The aftermath will cut off your nose.
I want to get rid of the farm.
The farm bothers me.

Every decent farmer needs a sack of meat.
Here I solemnly state that I ate the beetle because I'm
tired. We'll certainly soap ourselves.

Put this special cement here, such special
cement is expensive.
A wild piton, which fans itself on its stomach, peels the sun's

ear. A squirrel expands its belly for
eating. You're out of glue. Out of grubby liters of wine.
The Bhagavad Gita is sketched on a telegram.

Pontius and Pilate created thirty-one thousand
roses. The stroke is in the bread paste.
A yacht dormouse stores a fur hat.

The calf grows and weeps.
As if this isn't your boiler room,
it builds an extra boiler room.

Leaves fly off the trees, *mamacita*.
In May flowers hungry ants are
hungrier than hungry ants.

ONLY THE SUN AND YOU

Approach the wall.
Approach the stone.
Brush your face along the wall and stone.
The white ball is the ball of the sun.
Friends are seen with the eyes,
which still miss them today.
We carried God on our shoulders.
Both have a notch at the same height.
God shines on the earth.
You'll piss on me one day.

THE WARNING OF THE SPHINX

1.

White white night, burn the grass for me.
I rock in the corner amid the white lime, amid the white lime.
My lover is afraid that
he'll no longer be the boyfriend.

2.

A soul in a boat.
A hand on a shoal.

3.

The scarecrow with a yellow paw will
drench the white cube. And the feathers that
I'll stick in my hair.

4.

Stomach, white gammon.
Father, edge of meat.
Wethers slept on sacks that turned into
blue stones.

5.

In reserves,
with small movements of the head,
I discover land torn up by glaciers.
I return greenery to Paros.

6.

Will you come, Terrible?
I made you mead and rags from stubble.
Yellow ships will have to be sunk.
Come.

7.

To slobber over Job with gray velvet.

8.

A tiny magical boy marches
through the Pentagram's windows.
His fingers are buried in the sky
as if stuck in honey.

9.

Take off your hat!
You too, Maximum Turnout, Blue
Marauder.

10.

I'm an oaf.
I'm Pontus.
I'm your meat bone.

Thus you testify for the Face.

IT'S NECESSARY

I lost a dog. He had to go
straight and then ·
sideways. I also lost the gull

that was pecking my head and bringing
bouquets. All my life I fed
the gull so that it would crash into the glass

of the clock, scatter it, and eat it.
The gull betrayed me. Kittens are
corporeal. What should go in the story

with the brown fishing net is set
on the edge of a heated stove. I
obey only ample

curses. Every lump of coal
should be allowed to breathe.
You can eradicate what you invaded.

Frost forms on the mind. From there
it pulls roots into the water so that you'll
carry them on your back like sprouts.

It rows ontically, leaps over
the frayed fence. Pinocchio already
felt infinitely splendid in

the red mallet. I know the bats
have grown hairs, which I will
pluck and give to the Sisters of Mercy.

A BOX ABOVE THE SEA?

We're unearthed, we're unearthed.
We're unearthed, we're
unearthed. There are green peaches

in the fruit. I'm guarding the villa.
Consequence as a word comes from
the canal, not from rocks. Switchbacks

are extracted from rocks. From
hills sprinkled with salt,
many things. The creaking and dying

of birches. The birches cannot breathe because
of the salt. Birches don't grow in the hills.
Birches wear red shoes.

We're unearthed, this time
for real. We swim. The board that
triggered and opened dropped us into

the water. The board that was the roof of the hideout.
There were no scales. No scales when I swim
in the sea, unearthed and wet.

THE CLOUD OF UNKNOWING, P. 180

Go, go, because in the expertise beneath
the moss, there, where the tooth
of the blessed truly starts to swell, a bell

chimes. A gnat that catches fire
and strikes the clapper has no
chance. Have you ever encountered

rags soaked with honey?
Buttonholes are sewed alone again,
legs are spraying. I numb

an insect and attach it to my
body. I test how much a palm
hurts if you beat the surface with it

with all your might. Water is not
a henhouse. Salt's in it because
of hunger. Curtains aren't only on

a stage, some insufficiency always
squints there because the column rotated.
The sun illuminated it in a straight

line. In a straight and unstraight, in
the glare and at Špik. I take shelter. Let
Špik signify rush and reed and

sphere and shadow and factory and
even the preparation of Jacob and
the same one whose poultry goes to sleep

after her. Now I'm dreaming that
Machiavelli puts on felt sandals,
slides in them so as not to awaken us.

SHEETS

How and why does this brief prayer
pierce heaven? My ossicles crack,
my nose spreads like a peacock's tail.

They place lilacs in wet circles, utter
only one word: we're silk
and why is it honorable to divine the future

with sugar? Because it's not divination? Because
high tide opens your lips? The bee ceiling
swirls, the rug is made of spheres, they're soft,

they're wild, they're muscular, they're shy and
clueless. There are so many of them, they're like
a sea where we can't tell the difference between

a drop and a drop, a flap and a flap,
between difficulty and darkness. Kindling is
flat. Rolling and turning,

a deer poops on the hill. The horn is
as it will be, this is silence, how it is,
the fan is like that, as if it dwells between

ferns and milk cans on
the buses that go past.
There's still darkness. It's still not ringing. The folio

is a polyp. It lives in fat. It cries and
dances. It tramples ore and blood. From
the heights it tramples ore and blood. It meets

and consoles me. The cries are from the brushes'
brushes. So the deer's legs float and
the workers aren't going to work yet.

OLYMPIC EXEMPLAR

This morning a horse entered the room and
straw hauled itself after it. The horse

like an autonomous being. With eyelashes like
autonomous beings. With memories of

the lost. We put a zebra skin on the floor
for it. Why did you like her? Because she was

being written? The horse finished its meal and
complained a little about the neighbors'

munching. When? During the meal or during
the ringing of the bell? It didn't have time

during the ringing of the bell, I suppose it was during
the meal, and they took Ritsos from the plane

and hoped he'd whisper *this is Macedonia*.
The horse fidgeted with my grandfather's stamens.

VIVA ITALIA, WORLD CHAMPIONS, 1982

Look at how I'm putting my hand on my
throat. Look at the sign, how out of
nowhere there's a white spurt that dusts your
palm. You wait for the train. There is no train.
The train curves and tilts, the bell rings.
Does one have to put firewood on unwashed
skin? What to sacrifice in the cafe,
the hall of a skyscraper? A knot like
power. A knot like a bridge. A knot like
the center of the world and a cluster. It's a gnarl and it's
a plane. It's a gnarl and it's a plane. It's the Ganges.
Without rings and a bound chest.
And when the train moves, the poster
rustles again, the Ganges soaks the skin.

THE CREW

The Lord is silent in the tent, not at
lunch. The moth likes doing handsprings off
a piece of wood. When she's not stretching her neck,

she drinks. God brought her onto a ship on
His shoulders and then left her there.
She avoided the sailors. She gazed

at the sea with a rag. She looked through
the glass, which was thick. Did you
see the stroller? There are two strollers

in the sea. Blue and white.
Fish don't distinguish colors, so the moth
is protected. Bubbles open for

the fish. You almost never provoke the moth
during lunch. *Lieutenant! Lieutenant!*
The crew was replaced. The sea was

turning yellow and bloated.
The moth crashed into a strainer.
She was so thoughtful her entire

life. She missed the actual
dock. *Lieutenant! Lieutenant!* She didn't
understand. The crew was replaced.

BLOOD IS SPURTING FROM SOMEONE'S NOSE

The ox (like every other animal) treats
its boxes very religiously. The eagle-owl lives in
the mountains. The ox kills her. The vase was positioned

differently last time. In the painting there's
a girl in a slip with a shrub. The bridge
symbolizes meat. The bridge isn't in the painting.

When a young poet sits in an armchair and
stares at Metka's paintings, the figures in it start
to move. The pupils start to squeak over

the sugar. It's immediately covered by incense,
water, olive branches, and a congregation. Commissions
come. Commissions come

for centuries. The city is scorched; were there miracles?
In Lisbon you can sit on a bench with Pessoa.
The lower soul, the upper soul, start to crawl into the hills.

POEM

Where am I?
Where do my gallows stand?
Why do I have grainy eyes?
The town will follow you.

A crocodile crams my body into its tongue.
Is there some meaning in being left without
sorrow in the middle of artificial fires?
I vomit because I no longer have

sorrow. I get no
                    rest. I'm not
caressing your little body, Metka.
You're far away and the tongue is close.
It eats me in the herd.

It rolls over me like Hannibal with his donkeys,
I already emphasized the elephants too much,
I hope he also had donkeys.
My poetry hasn't been authentic
for a long time.

It rots from the glow alone.

HEARING

The desire to be quick clones me.
O how dark and heavy and quiet the bell is.
Uniform intervals soothe.
Why not say once quite simply
that I'm afraid of death?

IN THE MORNING

Infidels measure their prey by the length
of an oar. In every sea there's some
angel in a sunken bell.
One day the Pacific Ocean will vanish.
We're making a new Pacific Ocean.
It's an enormous task.
The heat is severe.
The weight of all this water quenches
a bit, but not enough. One
must use symbolism for the launching
of ships.
This pleases the meek.
Tomcat, kittycat, prey, shoo.
All my life I've been counting tiger teeth.

SIRENS

I blossom into shoulders.
I throw a horse's snowball into lingonberries.
Mold. Silkworm. A mouse leg scratches the slats.
Languishes and steps onto the deck of an ordinary ship.
It loosens the slats. Loosens the straps. Suns the leg.
It watches the splashing and sunbathes.

Like a worm that donates its body before it gets there—
it donates it somewhere, where it dissects—
like a worm that blots, bites and hears cymbals.
Is this why there's a tail?
Dolphins come and give rides.
Bestow wetness.
Which, flat, at a ninety-degree angle, waves in the snow
before saying goodbye for the last time.

HORSES

Myths are treated like eyelashes.
Both (some in twos, rocks between)

spurt, rivers spurt the most.
We live, we peel, we live,

the train rattles. Where does dust fall? Onto
an elephant's eye? There, where fish

spawn? Have irises ever shod
trains? We sang in a chorus. One

had spattered heels, one refused
heels. All the umbrellas were waiting to unfurl in the left

pantry. The women peeked through
nettles, the switchman fell asleep on

his side. We wrapped our own eyes in flannel
and bowled with them. Those were happy times.

MASTER

O, master of pharmacy, they cloned your
golden head, your greedy downcast

eyes. You are my God, I meet you
often. I'm drumdrumming your head

with a fan, I'd like you calm. I'm your
appetite, you're my appetite. I met four of you in

Salzburg. I have bait in my lap and I stick out
my legs. If I spilled a can of milk on you,

do you think I could save you? I'd delight
in this, how you poisoned us. We adore you,

Trakl. We're personally licking your hair.
I, I would prepare expenditures with bits

of your skin. On the plane we ate plump
mussels just like your plump heads.

NÄSSJÖ

White grass, did I call you?
If it's like this after death, it'll be boring.

Everything made of wood and in the forest. People
beautifully dressed. For breakfast, red

mountain-ash pomes, peacetime
pomegranates. The men in slippers, all

the women on ledges, barefoot. They all speak
Swedish and have yellow teeth.

They're respectful and pleasant and they beam and
their yellow teeth turn into white galvanized

sheet metal. The sand on the trails is volcanic.
They also hire snake tamers and it's still

boring. The women make Japanese
parasols. There's no soap. No bee. No sting.

UMBRELLA IN A BATHTUB

Slander the coffin so that it
falls apart. So that the corpse doesn't

look like some
sushi. Warn the owner that the castle will

burn down. That flesh will be
inhaled. That people will

throw towels and a trough from
the windows. Handles and

a trough. Alternating. Like Tesla's
current. Like a steamboat that breaks down

outside the mill.
Like a fox curled up

in the forest. Like a child who
steps on a stool and falls.

FIELD

Butchers are cold.
People with hoods are cold.

The clothed and the brittle are cold,
black and white.

We're alone.
We have mouths plump as

grasshoppers and
they beam.

Ash shakes.
A Frenchman breaks in with a mechanical

key and eats
strawberries.

Chess is pressure.
I'm as light as a curtain of foam.

PASOLINI

If a poem is a rainbow,
only a few degrees

are translatable. The sun must endure.
There's darkness before, there's darkness

after. The dog hears only
a certain sound. We don't talk about

the oaks, they hear with their eyes. But
there are no eyes. No trees. There was

a stream in the moss. When the corpse
burned, my jaw

twitched. I imagined
frayed ropes rushing

through a pulley in Damascus. A basket
full of dates and figs, and soapwort.

I DECIDED ON A WINNER

Come on, come on, sweetheart,
you're already an arsonist,

already a comma.
The emerald is an outfit,

it's a feathery boy,
it's a white ebb tide

without a mouth and face and
eyes. Gnocchi is in your

field. Just like
the semicolon. Just like

the colon
before the clause, the current

fashion with a bucket of water
in the soul.

WHEN THE HEART BURSTS

I overtake at dusk because I want to kill myself.
At the same time I'm deeply grateful for my whole

life. If I fall in love, my head bursts, a sad
novelty. I'm awake. I'm taking valium. As

a youth, I didn't dare. I wanted to be pure.
Even now I want to be pure. Making love is

beautiful, but terrible. Poetry doesn't contribute
to peace of any kind. It contributes to explosions and

pain. How it burns and crushes my chest, which might
seem humorous if dread and darkness didn't start

there. Love kills, today is a bright day. Everything
is pure. Snow melted wildly for three whole days.

I remember being disgusted with Jaša when
we learned: Tito visited his sister. His sister

offered him wine and Tito said, polish off this
plonk. The chauffeur opened a bottle for him. All

chauffeurs are terrible. All those who push my
poems into foreign languages, just like I tell them.

THE ACACIA

What about this girl, Caesar, who throws me into the babbling.
I also don't like Pound, he poisoned me, fish.
I'd like to be Juarroz, I'd like to be Braco, but

I'm not, so what, I'm such as life constructed
me, as light flooded me (yes, it's
me), as they kicked me like a lump and broke

my legs like an acacia. It sees me, hears me,
tempts my solitary walking off
the road. And in fact, the trace, I swear, wasn't

the wind, plants sometimes stir,
welcome you. *No hunting*, our walks are
the branches of stars. The sunflowers are resting,

but are you dust? I'm not, I'm green, I'm washed,
I'm washed, but you're falling, you're expanding, is it
dangerous? It's still not dangerous, I just

feel it. Love's grace hasn't glazed me
yet, a terrible thanksgiving. I remember
people's surprised looks before the night

broke me. Not the night. The cold. The gray, steely
cold. I shivered above the highway, a force shoved me
over the railing, I didn't want it, the force wanted it,

I was writing, I didn't know that I'd hurt myself
like this. That I'd penetrate. That there'd be no more
sun. That I'd be hurled there. Tires spray, tires

leave, tires lick, a fable, it'll still be a fable,
it'll exclude me, the river is life, it'll still be
a fable, the acacia sees this. The acacia warned me.

LILIES IN PROUST

I'm not my own bacterium,
I'm a foreign bacterium,
I'm a foreign bacterium with

its own identity, Saint Neža.
The lights are off.
Malta is iron.

I'm a barrel of brittle skies,
I hear a gasoline engine.
A monkey boils cubes. Not

bouillon cubes, ordinary cubes,
red, yellow, blue
plastic. How much boiling,

what temperature
does plastic withstand in water?
We'll see, find out and

report. The Scuola di San
Rocco admitted
the stooped, the maimed, and

the fetid.

TOPALČIKOV

Now I'm drawing Topalčikov, who's walking on
the road, not on the road, though also on
the road, it's for a link, no, a pier, no, for
a bond, a bond, I'd say,
a bond between two islands.

The lines are here.
The lines are here and the lines are here and the lines are here.
The circles are here.
The circles are here and the circles are here and the circles are here.
There are valleys and rocks and sand and sea.
Sparrows are here.
The sparrows are in my eyes.

It's warm here and the valleys are here and black soil is here.
The ships are pushing their propellers backward.
The lines on the sun are here.
The circles in the water are here.

SHEEP GATE

My smoothness scorched the feathers.
I was trying to build a cement cavern.
The pine demanded violet honeycombs,
a violet elderberry tree.
I'm a statue. Weariness covers my
eyelids. For goldfinches, smoothness
is lovely. In Copenhagen
I turned the bell around, broke through
the sand from below, alone, in the dark
with the clapper. Whoever rises early
gets on the boat. The leaves stretch my
bones and the gnats. Now I'm already in
magma, swimming. Close the window.
You're responsible. I'm the sheep gate.

CORINTHIAN COLUMN

The swamp birds are all soiled.
The swamp birds smash into the bark
with their bellies. We don't know
the lowlands. What's underground
isn't visible to the eye. If you walk on foot,
you calm down. Walk on foot. I dreamed that
the diamond cracked. The water
melted it. I dreamed that my ceramics
climbed the ladder in the barn. I marked
all the clamped lips with pins.
We'll wash the charcoal. It shouts the most
in the heels. If I opened my wings,
I'd cast a shadow on everything that
a shadow hasn't been cast on yet. Wander.

GASTARBEITER

Elsewhere, on Pohorje, I searched for
the frozen. We're made from
islets and hammocks. An enormous sage

leaf falls with a parachute. The soldiers
are happy animals leaning on
trees. I wrote my poems

with a whip and by splattering
ink on paper, just like everyone who
sleeps. The lightweight panties that I

ran away in startle the raven. It hasn't really
arrived yet. It looks at the buttons because it's
an addict. The wind sticks in its

feathers. Eventually it will topple over and
die, fall onto the road and commit suicide.
Yellow chanterelles similar to sacred mushrooms

will grow nearby. And substitute
buses will rush past without noticing
the corpse. May there be peace on earth.

CHECKERED CHRIST

He's viciously harassed. He has yellow elbows.
When hay gets on his tongue, he dies.

With white horses he delivers tentacles
to those who've been standing in line forever.

I'd like to eat a salad so that it flutters down my
throat. So that it flaps around my thorns, so that there's

a humane and soft axis to caress.
I'd like to melt an axe in a skillet. In a green

wheel, in a green coat.
My alarm clock is stinging. I uncovered

the vases. Florence was concealed by landfills.
The t-shirt is a biting red.

Luck! the river of quinine has emptied.
No one saw it at the window when washing the sills.

FUSION

Give me your eyes, give me your eyes, stop in front
of my eyes. At night it was strange. You boiled

my lungs. The fluid in them had turned
black, you were like three hundred thousand Persians

marching toward a dry
tree. You amalgamated me, shackled,

melted, shackled me again. The handle was despondent. There was
a storm. Green hydrochloric acid spilled

onto a hundred thousand ants. I didn't
interfere. Branches burned in an instant. Am I

snuffed? Am I alive? I saw a garden. Damp leaves
smoked like manure at first,

then moved, the giant's one eye
watching. It's true. I'm reckless. No longer.

"SHOULDER THE SKY, MY LAD, AND DRINK YOUR ALE"

Thinking in poetry is white iron
fertilized in a snake. The mountain roars, the fire

waits. Thinking in poetry is a sweater whose
threads are torn and a sprint swimmer.

This one touches the edge of the phallus pool and
wins. The battle is famous. The hands

are red. Flashes of lightning prepare the umbrella.
Thinking in poetry is the DAF, which fails

because the state doesn't defend it. O Dutchmen,
you cost me my reputation. The door is

black, the reptile has a beard. A finger licks
molasses, a wound in the sky. It sleeps and shakes

through the felt, shakes cubic meters of firewood. The sun
shines—the bee is red again—and sets.

CRIME AND PUNISHMENT, HANGED MEN

Victor Hugo was the most intelligent.
He drew his hanged man among birds,
very far from the ground.

From behind one sees a boat and how people
stare.

*

Hanged men are the most beautiful flowers.

Hanging must also spread to
kitchen assistants.

*

Why wouldn't Christ be hanged once
instead of dying on the cross.

At home the wife of the hanged man surely knits
something and moans.

*

Every hanged man has a dry head.

ADIEUX ADIEUX FRISETTE
(No exclamation point. He had to give the penknife
to another hanged man.)

*

Hanged men are disturbed if a river roars nearby.

Rouault understands the hanged man perfectly.
I'm surprised.

*

Indians are holding hands. Among
them are also hanged men.

*

It's hard to individualize the elements of a hanged man.
The bread and butter of a hanged man!

Every hanged man has his own milk
can.

*

Hanged men are teachable.
I see a three-year-old hanged man and I'm gentle.

The hanged men invited me to the dance, mother,
the hanged men.

*

Goya undresses one girlfriend,
I have no idea if he belongs among the hanged men.

Munch draws hanged men and a vulva.
Heart, you're a sack and ugly.

*

Hanged men are actually most similar
to butterflies.

THE MURDERER'S HAIR

A snake appeared and said: the cut
in your mouth is too deep,

I'll stitch it for you. The snake is a flower. The snake
isn't ash. If you want to kill people,

you must break worms first. A worm
must be hard so that you can break it

like a woody piece of asparagus. The snake
wasn't content with this. It dried its

shutters. Chet Baker spits on the floor, then
dies. In the dark wagon, no one noticed

him, we transported gold. Damp and frayed
rags made of jute were on the white heads.

Matryoshka, give me the Siberian
spirit, give me the Siberian *flavor.*

THE PLASTIC SURGEON SPEAKS

Blistered from carrying
furniture: lie down and rest.

With an open palm, wait for the carp.
It's coming soon. Louise explains

this beautifully: Brancusi's spine
is broken.

One roast hurled
through the window, two

octaves. All my life I
was greasy and

hardworking. I filed noses. With a file,
sometimes with a saw. I milled and

milled all my life, until
a miller married me.

DEAR SABA

I picture you in a large
gray tree in the desert,

how you sit quietly among the monkeys and
wonder. This has no association

with your Slovenian nanny.
Then I also see you,

how frost falls on your hair
and how you glisten.

My father was an alcoholic.
This isn't generally known.

He died when I was five
because he'd had

enough of life. The moon
shone, my dear Saba.

DEAR SABA

The clothespin will come. The clothespin
will undo me during the night. But

it lay you in wet sheets,
me in dry ones. All

your life you've been obsessed by the length
of your friends' penises, just like

every normal person who isn't
an ideologue. No one saw

Jesus Christ alive after
he died. I remember

the clatter of the stairs. My intention isn't that
readers go crazy when they read me,

my intention is for them to be unburdened.
I'm still far off.

DRULOVKA

The ostrich rocks the boat. Cuts
the ribbon. Inch by inch you move

away from the roof. At the clearing
where we camped. Where I

wanted to spend my youth with my
family. An oar buried itself

in the grass. What would you put on a carriage
if I could drive a carriage

here. The vault of your soul?
Your mess kit?

A trace of moss? Look through
the human head. It's not

the only one that has a groove. It oozes
from the sky. You gave away your eyes.

MILES AND MORE

Fairytale decadents, people with
wrinkles. Lift the deranged

animal. Grill her stomach. With blue
lips I chewed the dust that

already melted. Alexander was
shot when he'd already gone

into the little basket. I removed my head and
slowly wiped the counter with my wet

brow. People were sympathetic toward me,
also savage. Come with me,

come with me, he kissed me
and, God knows, gently begged

if he could slaughter me. Let me sunbathe
in front of the pillar, leader!

CRANIAL BASE

The cranial base expands. There
it flutters the shank. Washes it.

In a lake. In a pond. An eraser
or a belt more than

three kilometers long.
We're making all of this.

At the base little flowers
sprout. We can

turn them over and plant them
again. We

walk on the lake in
snowshoes until

the snowshoes sink. Night
buries itself in the sand.

MORNING

Immortality comes and goes, don't deceive yourself
young man. If you don't seize it by

the horns, it will look back. At the moon. At a theodolite.
It will only illuminate your paired

brain, paired heart, paired t-shirt,
paired eyes. Everything on you will be

hemmed, pressed, and creased. Hide
under the snow and rest. In the storm,

when I had to drop a barrel of oil into the sea
to make an eye, a blazing barrel,

immortality embraced you. Let it not be
for the last time. Dante doesn't report on this. Not

Ariosto, not Torquato Tasso. Grab
yourself by the sleeves and soar. Stay.

SURVIVAL TOOLS

The porter's face rolls like
a ball that will hit

a pin. The sun sets in a crack.
Mosques rustle. I received

a plastic red belt.
And a sheriff's badge.

Red coupons in God's ears—
also living eyes, living

eyes, living eyes. I embrace the hill
with my feet,

the pink beetle. The sun sets
in a crack. And:

my needles are sailing, sailing.
Happiness is a horn.

EVERY MORNING WE ROWED TOWARD THE HOLY SPIRIT

I seldom yielded to the pasha.
I remember that

fiery courtyard and the cattle
whose fence prohibited

access to the lake. Between the lake
and the fence you had

to move as if down a narrow
hallway even though there were

no walls. The sun was shining.
One could see intoxicated

branches enclosed by moss, and
you smell of skin and

not of sand. Bring
me milk and bread.

BENITO MUSSOLINI HAS HIS FINGERS IN HIS PANTS

The sheatfish emerges. *Adieu! Adieu!*
An egg white bursts if you toss it into a black nettle.

I was tricked by the cardinal, who looked
at me through paper. The mares—increasingly

rare—were touching. I know what I drive. I drive
cakes. With a boot I move the hill. *Merci,*

merci oozes from Beelzebub—he doesn't have
styrofoam in his voice. My machine:

a chicken, which is simultaneously a plank and
a chicken, is being staged alone. Moss

reclined and rustled. Pearls are
tangled in the carburetor. A whale lives in

the country. It has eyes supported by beams.
The eyelids are the mortar of its unborn sons.

GOOD FRIDAY

The oar spins like straw in a chicken's ass,
the parishioners have curly hair. I step over

the shards, a horse sleeps in the sound of rain.
A miser flees headlong.

Misers flee headlong.
The plane is frozen, the wood warms up.

I'm sure I have a clean shirt.
I took my leave under the blanket.

I was squeezed into Constantinople.
Tails touched my wet skin.

Job was counting teeth. Next to him stood:
the Sultan, a man with a white shako and white chalk

on his left shoulder who helped Job
count teeth, and another. It was already dark.

POWDER

A baby and animals are summoned during the meal.
When I crossed the Danube, I didn't see fish

because I was too high on the bridge.
A cork betrayed the mass murderer,

I knew the cork would betray him.
The pictures in the frames are little birds.

We smash the jungle with hammers.
Cut yourself down. Turn your head to the side.

When I walked on the flying carpet,
it crashed into the cans so that they clattered.

The powder on the cork betrayed the mass murderer,
I knew the powder would betray him.

QUIETLY CHANGING

You can inflate a mass murderer's legs
so that they'll be round as balloons, but he won't

notice. This is also the only way you'll track
him down. But where to get a pump? Where to get

a mass murderer? Mass murderers are
safely hidden around salons. If they steer

a cart up a hill, their facial muscles
tremble. I remember a mass murderer at

the camp in Visoko when I was fourteen.
He arranged cans of milk

on a small wooden cart. We talked.
He was from the village. On the left stood

a rectangular hayrack, and because darkness
was already falling, I didn't look him in the eyes.

MBUBE, ZULU FOR LION

Maybe I'll stop this pyrotechnics
and remember what it really was.

My prememory sponge kneels in the mud.
It has a wet bladder and golden wings.

My prememory sponge grabbed
the colt and the ore, opened the door. Lice

defecate. Lice defecate like people.
People cry. People cry like

people. Every fish freezes.
My warm fur departed.

To lose the bull. To varnish the spruce with
the mind, with the mind. Our shine, our sheatfish,

our food, our moisture, our sleeping
on our stomachs on a cart with the horror.

JOHNNY, WHAT ARE YOU TRANSLATING?

I burned the woods and my eyelids,
my eyelashes first, then my
eyelids. The mirror was a furious lake.

Threads were butchered at the bottom of the well.
Archaelogists lose the trace here.
Where were they standing? At the bottom of the well?

Beside the well? What help was the wool
if water seeped through? Were
the knitting needles bent? Let's forget. Let's close

(cover) the well with an old, rotten
board. I don't want to peer inside. My neck hurts
from sniffing. From the bliss of the land mines

that I carry under my skin. There are dewdrops,
the ascension of cumin, and then I hear my
sandals, I hear an island, the piece of leather under my

sole, somehow under the mound that is
connected with the spleen and the wooden door decorated
with garlands. The liver doesn't have a wooden door

decorated with garlands. Shintoism is like
cocaine. A drug for pharmacists and
attorneys, not for brutes. For brutes there's

only poetry. I saw that beetles with
dark green armor started to lift weights. Salt
sweetens them under the sea. Horses away!

THE LAKE

Wisteria rip the tarp off the monkey's chest
with large wheels and great force. The camp gazes
into the valley. Bends. Gray birds thunder

at the hypothesis of cells. I have no idea when the valley
was submerged. Maybe three hundred thousand
seventy-two years ago. I saw

a postman. He was swimming out of the house. His
bag was rolling in yellow water. Smoke
came from the chimneys. I didn't understand how

smoke lives underwater. How the postman breathes.
How daisies and clover retain their
color. How the seasons don't

collapse beneath the poster. Where the postman changes
his clothes. Why he doesn't sleep in a trunk. Why he has
shorter legs than the other postman, his

colleague. A pine needle fell on the surface
of the lake. It's already traveling. Already soaking
in the water and rushing toward the postman's head.

MOLLUSK

I'm a mollusk.
Bound with hooks.
Ironed by

motor
vehicles, no? I ask
hunger

to watch me,
I ask hunger to turn
away.

Why would I
graze when the Lord
looks at me,

who else
grazes when the Lord
looks at him.

BONE

The battle is ceremonial,
the cities' feathers
are ruffled.

Orpheus
bleeds from the mouth and
hair.

A marble drenched
a willow and then
an olive tree.

Newts still close their eyes without
eyes. Štefka was
naked.

She breathed
slowly, the moon,
which smelled of sand, fell

on her. They put
a helmet
made of chains

on my head
so the bees wouldn't
sting me.

THE FAMILY AT DINNER

A serial killer doesn't belong in
a serial sack. A serial

killer is focused, sober,
velvety. He doesn't wash his

hands, he doesn't wash his feet, he doesn't wash
anything. He lies in the grass and

listens to Baloković, who's playing
in the moonlight under

the triumphal arch. What is he dragging?
A flag, grass,

a boxwood, a cabbage? All of it. All of it.
All of it at once. A snack and

a dried pork neck and the banging of the sea's waves
and the forks in the bowls.

PEASANT UPRISING

We would, but
we can't.

Gentlemen scratch our
cheeks. Out of the canvas

came a symbolic mother and
bowling. Black parquet.

Parquet is always wood.
I filled a thunderous wall

with fermented shit. Nothing
special. Manet

died relatively young. In Warsaw
we ate pine nuts. People

gawk at simple things and
I am simple.

THE SPINDLE MAY NOT COME IN THE WINDOW

The Carmelites are barefoot.
The spindle fears the peacock.

The Carmelites grab a blue sheet,
raise it overhead and roar.

I am a Carmelite! I
am a Carmelite! All four of them. At

all four corners. Then they stream
barefoot over soft grass with the taut blue

sheet. They set it down on the grass.
Their feet gush.

Gurgling is heard. They're no longer
Carmelites, immersed in water.

They weep and become dried
chamomiles, regardless.

My small bones love
your small bones.

A tremendous feeling.
Flowers grow above us.

People stomp.
Some have wet shoes.

They light candles and smack their lips.
They're attractive. Our

small bones—entire little owls.
If you dig them out of

the ground, they frighten
no one. They're sacred

bones. Ossa sacra,
mamma mia.

PRESERVE, PRESERVE

I forge you with leather
straps. The iron is

hot, the salt blows. Stabat Mater
with fluff. Here, too, with

a green net. With green
eyes. You have millions

of lips. Waterfalls, ledges with
jaguars. A jaguar comes

up to me, personally, wants
to tell me something. There

were two sisters. They took
us from the snow, immersed us

in the jungle. We never
ate hearts again.

SKIN PRESERVATION

I undressed him behind the mummies.
His clothes slid silently

off him. Beside the pillar, at
sunrise.

In the church. The mummies
banged. The mummies

in Vodnjan rejoiced and
informed the mummies in

Guanajuato. Here, too, we have
moons, constellations, a city

underground. My paw
floats. Here, too,

we have a white cap, a white visor,
we make love with the sun.

TROUT

Breath pushes into a heap and thickens
the blood. Humanity's billions

sleep. Horses! It's a little bird!
We quarrel, where is the water.

What is water, who has dry
hair. Destroyers!

Roving. The pharaoh had
bullfinch eyes, red

murky colors. A wolf munches with
its teeth. The wind was

caught in the branches. This is
prose! yelled

the boy. All were astonished.
I hatched an egg.

SALT THAT BOILS

I had a modern structure and
a carpentry workshop.

The path went from the heart toward
the skin. I upset

the guards. I upset the firefighters on
the towers. White white wax,

the neck beneath the bird carries a bundle.
They built the bells with

trucks. The workers. With
bandanas around their heads. With

stamps on the soles and young
nurseries.

The earth is round.
It was never flat.

BUTTONS

A green tale of gunfire.
A yellow tale

of gunfire. It pricks with a needle.
I'm devouring grass.

In the slaughterhouse they separate skin from
the body. They stuff

candy into the mouth.
Mama comes.

Sister comes, too. They walk
around the park in

sandals. It's drizzling gently and
life is

black and gray. With skin
suspended over a pipe.

COOING KNOCKS DOWN PALM TREES

I imagine my mouth stretched out
for the last time on this mountain.

Flower driver—joy in a helmet.
Flower driver—a man on

handlebars. An old man drives
up the stairs, the hill

strives for the street.
The chains are

coated with sparrowhawks,
Schopenhauer's

lake. I'm going to sleep now.
I'm going into the earth

now. O, cherries! The universe
favors you.

SKIN

My skin evaporated like some
bandleader's. It babbled in

tin sacks. If I were born
again, I'd babble. Babble in water,

beneath the roof, on a raft. I'd babble by
the plump blue daisy in the air

and extend my hands to chimpanzees. In India
I was once teased by one

(a monkey), then I went to a Belgian
bank and stood there with other

people on the stairs until it opened.
My skin evaporated like

some bandleader's. I wander, wander,
wander your sea.

THE BEACH

I never learned to turn on
pagodas. Teeth

peel, teeth fall out. It's
up to you, it's

up to you. We burned
the cloak late last

night. I took them in
my palm and blew on them.

Maybe they rolled over, but
they gave no

reply. They advised
a quartet, but

I went with nine. They called
me a subcutaneous pearl.

SYNTHESIS OF DAY AND NIGHT

Nudity was invented
by the British.

Their mothers are
without nudity.

Do you see how they're
covered?

A synthesis of day and night.
The rupture is when

Tiresias grew his first
nipple and then

the Holy Spirit
ricocheted and

lurched around inside
a gas pipe.

THE SKIN OF THE APPRAISERS IS COVERED WITH
BLACK FLIES

If I had three bits of bread,
I'd toss out

the first when the train crosses
the Soča. For the second,

I'd pretend that
I forgot it on

a bench. I'd turn the third
in my hands,

raise it during the ride.
Chains are

attached to the trees.
The bread booms.

The bread breaks. Devastation
is unnatural.

SOMEONE BY A FROZEN LAKE

From moment to moment
we'd grind truth and grain and

grass and coffee. And why, why?
I went through a girded

country. The fishermen slapped
columns. The sun banged,

covered up, but banged again.
Burned paper lay

in the streets. With my left
middle finger I

removed the sleep from my right
eye. I didn't stop

writing. Only now, when
I raise a glass of water.

The publication of this poem in the journal *Perspektive* led to Šalamun's arrest when a Communist official, Ivan Maček, interpreted the dead cat (*maček*) in the poem as a reference to him. Although Šalamun spent only five days in jail, the ensuing international outcry saw him emerge from jail as a cultural hero. Despite (or perhaps because of) this, he did not want to include the poem in any of his books and had to be convinced to include it in his 2011 volume of *Selected Poems* in Slovenia. I have included the poem here because of its historical significance.

DUMA 1964

Fucked by the Absolute
full of virgins and others mortally injured
I love you o neighbors, tame imagination of God the father
I love you o complete personalities of sweet regarding
in my soul mercy stirred
   o possessors of mental anguish
   o trained intellectuals with sweaty hands
   o logicians vegetarians with a -15 prescription
   o rectors with muzzles
   o ideologues with whorish ideologies
   o doctors ruminating on Škofja Loka bread and punctuation
   o mummies academically patting passion and pain
   Pascal who tried hard and Bach who succeeded
   o unspeakably deliciously drying up lyricists
   o enlightened horticulture and swallows
   o socialism à la Louis XIV. or how to protect poor little animals
   o one hundred thirty-five constituent bodies or what would you
   do with a dead cat so it wouldn't stink
   o the revolutionary nature of the masses or where is the sanatorium
   that would cure our impotence
I walked our earth and got a stomach ulcer
the land of the Cimpermans and their pimply admirers
the land of farmhands myths and pedagogy
   o flinty Slovenes, cold-ridden object of history

These are among Šalamun's last poems, which remain unpublished in Slovenia. Šalamun composed them in Bled, Slovenia, in September 2014, after he had been released from the hospital when the doctors could do nothing else to treat his cancer. Because he could no longer write or type, he dictated his final poems (forty-five total) to his wife, Metka Krašovec.

BLACK OVAL SHAPES

I'm bareheeled and also not bareheeled,
I see the whiteness of the church wall.
Ignore the gentleman with the hat, the gentleman with
the hat turns into death.
The gentleman also gargles.
He grinds his eyes
and arranges them. The apricots remain
in his palms. Would we try to order
something? If gasoline is spilled only on
the windbreaker, does only the windbreaker burn?

WHO IS PORCELAIN

And whoever directs the process with an open
mouth will summon a brown glass in vain.
The beans are scattered under the truck.
The opening fuels the sound. Because I'm beautiful and blue
and juicy and large. Horsehair in algae.
And who is porcelain? There's nobody here who'd
be porcelain.

NOTES

CAR LE VICE

"Car le Vice, rongeant ma native noblesse" is from Stéphane Mallarmé's poem "Angoisse." The phrase means "For vice, gnawing my native nobility."

KLUTZES

"My vocabulary did this to me" are the final words of the American poet Jack Spicer.

DEAR METKA!

"Dalmatinova" is the name of the street in Ljubljana that Šalamun and Metka Krašovec lived on.

ACKNOWLEDGMENTS

Many thanks to the magazines that published some of these translations:

Agni
American Poetry Review
Apartment
Barrow Street
Bat City Review
The Believer
Bennington Review
Blackbird
Boston Review
Broadkill Review
Changes Review
Circumference
Colorado Review
The Common
Conduit
Copenhagen
Copper Nickel
Crazyhorse
Cutbank
Denver Quarterly
The Drift
Epiphany
Fence
The Georgia Review
Guernica
Gulf Coast
Image
Interim
Jabberwock Review
The Journal
The Kenyon Review
Lana Turner
The Laurel Review
Los Angeles Review

Michigan Quarterly Review
Mississippi Review
The Missouri Review
The Nation
New American Writing
New England Review
The New Humanist (UK)
North American Review
Notre Dame Review
Ocean State Review
Octopus
Oversound
Plume Poetry
Poetry
Poetry Daily
Poetry London (UK)
Poetry Northwest
Poetry Review (UK)
Portland Review
Prairie Schooner
A Public Space
The Rupture
Sand Journal (Germany)
Scoundrel Time
Sixth Finch
Sonora Review
Southern Indiana Review
Typo
Volt
Volume Poetry
Washington Square
Witness
The Yale Review

I'd like to thank Miha Maurič and Aleš Šteger for their assistance from the very beginning, when this book was just an idea, and for their help deciphering some of Šalamun's more resistant phrases; Katja Lenič Šalamun for granting me permission to translate the poems in this book; the Interlibrary Loan office at Boatwright Memorial Library for tracking down copies of Šalamun's Slovenian books that I didn't already have; everyone at Milkweed who helped bring this book into the world; and Tara Rebele, Brynne Rebele-Henry, and Dara Barrois/Dixon for their support.

TOMAŽ ŠALAMUN was born in 1941 in Zagreb, Croatia, and raised in Koper, Slovenia. He is the author of more than fifty books of poetry, and his work has been translated into more than twenty-five languages. A curator and conceptual artist prior to becoming an acclaimed poet, his honors include the Prešeren Award, the European Prize for Poetry, the Mladost Prize, the Jenko Award, and a Pushcart Prize. He served as Cultural Attaché to the Slovenian Embassy in New York and, in addition to serving as a Fulbright Fellow at Columbia University, held various visiting professorships across the United States. He died in Ljubljana, Slovenia, in 2014.

BRIAN HENRY is the translator of Tomaž Šalamun's *Woods and Chalices*, as well as Aleš Debeljak's *Smugglers* and six books by Aleš Šteger, most recently *Burning Tongues: New and Selected Poems*. Henry is also the author of *Permanent State*, ten other books of poetry, and the prose book *Things Are Completely Simple: Poetry and Translation*. His work has received numerous honors, including two NEA Fellowships, the Alice Fay di Castagnola Award, a Howard Foundation fellowship, and the Best Translated Book Award. He lives in Richmond, Virginia.

milkweed
EDITIONS

Founded as a nonprofit organization in 1980, Milkweed Editions is an independent publisher. Our mission is to identify, nurture, and publish transformative literature, and build an engaged community around it.

Milkweed Editions is based in Bdé Óta Othúŋwe (Minneapolis) within Mní Sota Makhóčhe, the traditional homeland of the Dakhóta people. Residing here since time immemorial, Dakhóta people still call Mní Sota Makhóčhe home, with four federally recognized Dakhóta nations and many more Dakhóta people residing in what is now the state of Minnesota. Due to continued legacies of colonization, genocide, and forced removal, generations of Dakhóta people remain disenfranchised from their traditional homeland. Presently, Mní Sota Makhóčhe has become a refuge and home for many Indigenous nations and peoples, including seven federally recognized Ojibwe nations. We humbly encourage our readers to reflect upon the historical legacies held in the lands they occupy.

milkweed.org

Milkweed Editions, an independent nonprofit literary publisher, gratefully acknowledges sustaining support from our board of directors, the McKnight Foundation, the National Endowment for the Arts, and many generous contributions from foundations, corporations, and thousands of individuals—our readers. This activity is made possible by the voters of Minnesota through a Minnesota State Arts Board Operating Support grant, thanks to a legislative appropriation from the arts and cultural heritage fund.

Interior design by Mary Austin Speaker
Typeset in Adobe Caslon

Adobe Caslon Pro was created by Carol Twombly
for Adobe Systems in 1990. Her design was inspired by
the family of typefaces cut by the celebrated engraver
William Caslon I, whose family foundry served
England with clean, elegant type from the early
Enlightenment through the turn of the
twentieth century.